AF327185

37 DESIGN & ENVIRONMENT PROJECTS

First Annual Review

Text by Edward K. Carpenter

Introduction by Jonathan Barnett

Forward by Ann Ferebee

Published by R.C. Publications, Inc.
Washington, D.C.

First Annual Review

Copyright © 1976 by RC Publications, Inc. All rights reserved

Published by RC Publications, Inc.
6400 Goldsboro Road N.W.
Washington, D.C. 20034

No part of this publication may be reproduced or used in any form or by any means—graphic, electronic, or mechanical, including photocopying, recording, taping or information storage and retrieval systems—without written permission of the publisher.

Manufactured in USA

First Printing 1976

37 Design & Environment Projects
First Annual Review

Library of Congress Catalogue Card Number 75-24226
ISBN 0915734-08-7

RC Publications
President and Publisher: Robert Cadel
Vice-President and Editorial Director: Martin Fox
Editor: Ann Ferebee
Art Director: Emil Micha
Editorial Assistant: Ellen-Jane Opat
Design Assistant: Mark Weibolt

New Roles and New Clients

by Jonathan Barnett

In spite of the theories and aspirations of the design and planning professions, the total effect of our efforts has proved to be a great deal less than the sum of its parts.

A small number of buildings have received special attention: "prestige" headquarters of major corporations, institutional buildings financed by a donor—and, occasionally, by the taxpayer—or the homes of wealthy people. Most other structures are routine at best. It is true that architects work on them, but the real decisions are made by others; and, to put it kindly, the architects concentrate on solving technical problems rather than the larger issues of design.

An analogous statement can be made about civil and environmental engineering. There has been some outstanding work: great bridges, beautifully planned highways, but the general level is nowhere near the standard set by the best.

Recently, architects and engineers have come to realize that raising the design level of individual structures is only part of the problem. Even if each were designed by a master, the improvement in our everyday environment would not be significant unless some way were also found to design the relationships among these separate structures, as well as their relationship to the environmental context.

The planning and landscape architecture professions, which have understood this problem for a somewhat longer time, have not been able to provide any sure way of implementing coordinated development.

Central Design Issue

The problem of improving our environment, the physical surroundings that we live with every day, is the central design issue of our time. It far outweighs questions about the appearance of an individual building or a work of engineering. In fact it is becoming hard to remember why certain stylistic questions were once considered important. Why was it heresy to use ornament on a building? Why was it so terrible if the structure were not clearly expressed?

"Modern" architecture has become the norm, and we can see that it did not bring with it the expected style, or vernacular, which would restore the innate relationships that we see in buildings of the eighteenth century. It is clearly impossible to achieve such a simple kind of environmental coherence in our complex technological society. In fact, now that we all live in what Harold Nicolson called a "Woolworth world," some of those Neo-Gothic and Neo-Georgian buildings of the twenties and thirties are beginning to look quite good in retrospect. Many of them are far more sensitive to environmental considerations than their "modern" counterparts, whose architects were so busy expressing structure and internal arrangement that they forgot to look beyond the building line.

Environmental design requires that the designer be involved in a much larger context than that provided by his traditional role, but he can not expect to act with his accustomed authority in all of these new areas. He must learn to work with quite different professionals, and respond to unusual criteria.

Three Main Players

The three main players of the environmental game are government, with its dual role as regulator and builder; the real estate industry, which initiates the great majority of new buildings; and communities, including both local interest groups and national consumer lobbies. The design professional must learn to understand the working mechanism and priorities of all three, if he is going to be able to intervene successfully in the design of the environment.

DESIGN & ENVIRONMENT'S first awards for Excellence in Environmental Design show that design professionals are beginning to have some positive effect on the environmental context. This book, describing the 37 winning projects, is evidence that the design professional is learning to assume new roles and to operate in realms that have been closed to him up to now. Of course, these projects are only indicative. As you look out the airplane window, or drive down the highway, it is obvious that we are still a long way from a designed environment.

The awards are divided into three categories, each of which has two sub-categories. Inevitably these categories are somewhat arbitrary, and several projects could as easily be in one as another, but the topics cover important issues.

However, it is also instructive to look at these projects in terms of the three categories of client groups: government, the real-estate industry and communities.

Real estate is not strongly represented, although it is in many ways the area where the results of the awards program are the most encouraging. NewMarket at Head House Square in Philadelphia, page 62, Butler Square in Minneapolis, page 40, and the Galleria in New York City, page 60, are all expected to succeed in the market place without any special grant or subsidy. In fact, the qualities that make them worthy of awards should also enhance their competitive position against other real-estate developments.

In the case of Galleria, however, the Awards Panel has recognized the fact that the building would not have been possible without alterations to the New York City zoning regulations that were designed to encourage just such a result. Another heartening aspect of these awards is that they indicate a growing awareness of the strong role played by government in creating the built environment. In many instances governments are specifying through regulations almost exactly the result that then occurs, often without being aware that the environment produced is a direct response to the rules. Alterations to the rules, whether they cover electric transmission lines or apartment houses, can effect immdiate improvements in the environment.

Government as Builder

Government in its role as the builder of what are often categorized as "public improvements" is also strongly represented in these awards. It is encouraging to find public improvements that are really improvements. Governments account for a considerable percentage of the construction that occurs every year, and changes in governmental policies governing their own construction programs can also effect the environment favorably.

The idea that communities are somehow separate from the governments that represent them may seem strange; but, in a complex, bureaucratic age, we have to accept the fact that governmental institutions are not always immediately responsive to what large segments of their public really want. The battles over highway routes in recent years are good examples of the conflict between governmental and community interests.

The Report to the City of San Diego, page 12, embodying as it did a serious effort to inform the community about complex planning and environmental issues, is one way to deal with such conflicts before they occur. Another is a project like the Cleaves Court Apartments in Boston, page 82, which dealt sympathetically with the existing social context of the neighborhood, and not just with numbers of housing units rehabilitated.

Again, the results of this awards program show what can be done by the exercise of forethought and ingenuity, when design professionals are given the opportunity to deal with large-scale issues. What we must all work for, however, is the day when such awards are no longer necessary, because the projects represented here will have become typical rather than exceptional.

37 Projects that Work

by Ann Ferebee

When the editors of DESIGN & ENVIRONMENT invited readers to submit entries to a Program of Awards for Excellence in Environmental Design, we found the winning entries so unusual that we decided to devote a book to them. Aside from the inherent interest of the 37 winners, many are important because they call attention to aspects of the environment heretofore neglected in design awards programs. For example, the first seven projects focus on the natural, rather than the built, environment and on what designers are doing to preserve it. Among the projects to be cited, two are education programs: a National Forest landscape management program, page 18, and a program to educate state officials on preserving the beautiful backroads of Vermont, page 14. Lewiston Artpark, page 16, designed by the innovative New York architectural firm of Hardy Holzman Pfeiffer preserves and reclaims some 187 acres of land that had been rendered virtually useless from the dumping of chemicals.

The remaining projects, all dealing with the built, mostly urban, environment, are unusual in that, often, they include management, zoning or financing concepts beyond the scope of architecture, *per se*. For example, Gaylord Freeman, board chairman of the First National Bank of Chicago, is credited with inaugurating a program of free public activities for the bank's handsome new plaza, page 24. By focusing attention on the activities program, the Awards Panel emphasizes that environmental management, as well as architecture, is important in the creation of successful public spaces. The Galleria, page 60, was selected because of the stunning quality of the glass-encased public space. Equally important is the new zoning ordinance that permits mixed residential and commercial use in the Galleria. With its 252 residential units, the Galleria will make an important start toward keeping populated a mid-town New York area that, heretofore, had emptied out at the end of the working day.

Some of the most important projects are trend-setting in that they encompass an entire web of components within the urban infrastructure rather than a discrete segment of architecture. For example, at the gigantic Battery Park City Housing Development now under construction on land-fill in New York's Hudson River, it is not the buildings themselves that promise to be especially design worthy but the humane and sensitive open space plan, page 22, that calls for boutiques, street furniture, pedestrian bridges and fountains, among a host of other amenities.

One characteristic of many architectural awards programs is that they commend projects that are still on the drawing board or very recently completed. This practice has encouraged a deafness on the part of architects to remarks about buildings after they are built—by the people who live or work in them. To encourage architects to evaluate their work in terms of user satisfaction, we made Lived-in Environments a special category of our awards program. Then we encouraged comments from occupants who lived in the projects in this category and, where possible, sent editors to visit them. We found, in the case of Townoaks Townhouses, for example, that architectural design was an important factor in encouraging whites to move back into a racially balanced neighborhood that was fast becoming preponderantly black. For details on how the architect brought this off, see page 78.

Like Townoaks, Cummings Building, page 84, and Cleaves Court Apartments, page 82, are more socially than architecturally innovative. In both cases renovation was accomplished without losing the original tenants, thus helping preserve and maintain a fragile inner-city neighborhood.

With building starts slow and financing of new construction difficult, the preservation of old becomes increasingly attractive to the general public as well as to design professionals. What is interesting about winning entries in the category of Preservation is that they are widely varied—ranging from a gas utility complex, to a railroad station to a turn-of-the-century pier. Whether in the category of preservation, urban design or environmental enhancement, each of the 37 case studies that follow provide design, zoning or management techniques that are new—more important they really work.

ENVIRONMENTAL ENHANCEMENT

We believe that thoughtful intervention by the designer, planner or landscape architect can enhance both urban and rural environments. Therefore, we have divided projects in this division into two categories: those that preserve the natural landscape and those that enhance the cityscape.

Preservation of Natural Landscape

Design Guides for Electric Transmission and Substations, Southern California

Client: Southern California Edison

Designer: Henry Dreyfuss Assoc., Niels Diffrient, partner in charge; James Ryan, associate; Valerie Pettis, graphics

Citation: In recognition of the high quality of two design guide books that are the basis of an effective equipment design program and also for management policy, which accounts for the environmental impact of transmission routes.

Southern California Edison's concern with the appearance of its overhead transmissions towers dates back to the early '60s. In 1961 Henry Dreyfuss Associates designed a sunburst arrangement of pole head arms (to keep power lines separated) to be mounted on gray, stained-wood poles. Since then, Southern California Edison has installed several thousand of these in metropolitan areas. Next steps were the design of steel and concrete poles and either the enclosure or redesign of several complete transmission facilities (by Dreyfuss Associates and others). But it became apparent that this kind of piecemeal treatment was not enough. Needed were guidelines and policies to ensure that routes and sites were sympathetically studied by management.

"We felt," Niels Diffrient of Dreyfuss Associates said recently, "for a utility company to make decisions that modified the environment the following were needed:
(1) An understanding of what aesthetics meant in the context of their operation;
(2) Comprehension of the scale of impact their decisions had on the environment;
(3) Appreciation of how their equipment modified the environment;
(4) Understanding of their particular region and how it influences decisions;
(5) A consistent approach to design to avoid visually unrelated and random facilities; and a
(6) Communication medium which sets forth company policy on aesthetics and environmental influence."

Out of common desire to answer the above needs came the two *Design Guides* cited by the jury. "Aesthetic Guidelines for Electric Transmission" and "Aesthetic Guidelines for Substation Facilities" are not complete environmental handbooks, but they show with remarkable clarity and detail how powerlines can be pleasing and how electrical transmitting stations screened or unscreened can be a welcome part of their surroundings. "Southern California Edison Company," writes senior vice president Robert N. Coe, "is committed to an active program of aesthetic improvement."

Greene Valley Recreational Hill Development Project, Chicago, IL

Client: Forest Preserve Distric of DuPage County, IL

Designer: Waste Management Inc., Oak Brook, IL

Citation: For creative dumping. This program utilizes DuPage County solid waste to create the largest ski hills in the metropolitan Chicago area. The program provides badly needed space for a growing quantity of solid waste, while increasing recreational facilities by using the waste to create ski hills.

In October, 1974, trucks started dumping solid waste collected in DuPage County, on a 180-acre treeless site in the Greene Valley Forest Preserve. Eventually, in five to eight years, the refuse will make a 25000-foot hill, two of them in fact, mini mountains, which will be developed with ski lifts and toboggan runs for 3,000 of the more than half a million county residents.

Consulting landscape architect Donald Rippel prepared a master plan for the entire 1,453-acre Greene Valley Forest Preserve, and the ski hills will be but part of a collection of badly needed recreational facilities. Just as important, the county will be able to dispose of from 3,000 to 4,000 cubic yards of wastes a day until the hills are completed. Once the sanitary land fills have reached the proper contours, earth scooped from what will become a nearby lake, will be trucked to cover the refuse and provide a base for planting. This system has already created a 140-foot ski hill at the Blackwell Forest Preserve, also operated by the DuPage County Forest Preserve District, and the District plans a third development at the Mallard Lake Forest Preserve in the northern part of the county.

Actual operation of the land fills is the province of a private firm, Waste Management, Inc., which operates 55 sanitary land fills on 6,000 acres in 16 states and Canada.

Rendering (top), done once the design concept had jelled, gives an impression of the final towers (bottom). Scale model (middle), constructed once design drawings were complete, gives an amazingly accurate representation of a final installation.

San Diego has one of the U.S.'s most beautiful harbors (opposite). Maps above show suggested transportation routes (ferries, bikes, feeder buses, horse and walking trails), and suggested saving of valleys and mountains for enjoyment of everyone.

Temporary Paradise? A Report to the City of San Diego, CA

Client: City of San Diego, CA

Designers: Donald Appleyard; Kevin Lynch

Citation: In recognition of a successful regional reconnaissance of San Diego and an evaluation of its assets and liabilities. This unusual planning document was circulated as a newspaper to 50,000 citizens, informing them about, and drawing them into, the process of planning for the city's future.

Professors Kevin Lynch and Donald Appleyard have given San Diego a sort of pre-planning plan. This careful preliminary look at the city by two professional outsiders was printed up in tabloid newspaper form and distributed to 50,000 of the area's residents. From it, the town officials are getting reactions, suggestions, criticism and ideas for what will become definite plans for the city's future.

Lynch, of course, is professor of city planning at the Massachusetts Institute of Technology, and Appleyard is professor of urban design at the University of California, Berkeley. Their expertise is constantly apparent in the report.

Given the type of assignment, they could think grandly, and their suggestions are, as a result, always just what should be done, not necessarily what can be done. What will be left of their report once it has filtered through the years of surveys, inventories, plans and legislative hassle ahead is hard to guess.

Probably their most controversial suggestion is that San Diego consider planning for future growth with Tijuana, across the border in Mexico. "Treat San Diego/Tijuana as one unified metropolis," says the report, and judging from initial reaction in San Diego not everyone is ready for that kind of international cooperation.

Elsewhere the report suggests the formation of an Environmental Planning and Design Section in the city's planning department. This section would produce a plan for San Diego's environmental quality and encourage other departments to do the same. Ideally, this plan would deal with six basic values: livability, access, sense of place and time, responsiveness, pleasure and sensibility, and conservation.

Among the principles it backs are to: (1) begin to manage the environmental quality of the entire region in a coherent, effective way; (2) save the shorelines, bays, valleys and mountains and restore them to everyone; (3) retard suburban development and change its form to one better adapted to the site; (4) redirect growth of the existing urban neighborhoods; (5) reduce dependence on the automobile; (6) flatten the north-south social gradient and exploit the east-west natural one; and (8) conserve water, energy and land.

In a technical appendix submitted with their report, the consultants wrote: "Environmental quality is a principal motive for controlling growth, and policies for the location and character of development are key elements in any growth strategy. Thus, an environmental plan will be a basic element in any growth study, although it will not be the only element."

Local businessman and civic leader Hamilton Marston initiated the study. A "reconnaissance" is what he wanted, a survey of San Diego's strengths and weaknesses and suggestions for the regional future. Marston has lived in San Diego all his life. His grandfather, George Marston, founded a department store there (sold by the family in the '50s), and in 1908 he hired landscape architect John Nolen, fresh from Harvard, to draw up the city's first master plan. Following that lead, Hamilton Marston and his aunt put up the money to have a contemporary survey done. "It would not be intended to be a plan," said Marston, "but a body of information, a notebook of written comments and graphic sketches on the existing development of San Diego with observations and suggestions for the design of our city and the uses of our natural setting." It was Marston's idea to make the report broadly available.

The Vermont Backroad, VT

Client: Ottauquechee Regional Planning and Development Commission in Woodstock, VT

Designer: Robert F. Longfield, Jr., landscape architect

Citation: An imaginative effort in environmental education aims at preserving the backroads of Vermont, which provide perhaps the pleasantest motoring in the U.S. today.

Lovely as they are, Vermont's backroads (opposite) can be made even more so. Above top is a road before widening and clearance to improve views of fields beyond (bottom).

Almost every county in Vermont is laced with backroads, usually dirt or gravel surfaced, that wind through the countryside past fields and streams, through woods, offering supurb views of mountains and valleys. You can't travel very fast on them, nor should you want to, but as population increases so does the pressure to have them paved. Recognizing these backroads as a regional asset, the Ottauquechee Regional Planning and Development Commission sponsored preparation of a book that outlines how these roads can be modified, straightened a little here, widened a little there, without ruining, and perhaps even enhancing, the environment they pass through. Paid for by funds from the Woodstock Foundation and the Eva Gebhard-Gourgaud Foundation, the book is the work of landscape architect Robert F. Longfield, Jr., and in it he goes into some detail, accompanied by photographs and drawings, on how to do everything from run a road up a hill to improve views and drainage along it. For example, rule number four in the section on grading reads: "On areas of extreme cut, the use of small benches, stepped down a steep slope, will slow water runoff and provide excellent take hold. It is important to maintain a slight downhill pitch on these benches to provide adequate drainage." Accompanying rule four is a simple drawing showing the right and wrong ways of stepping down a slope. The book is a model of clarity, a complex subject made manageable and readily understandable. In appendecies are lists of grasses, shrubs and wildflowers that can stand the conditions along these backroads.

The foundations paid for mailing the report to the selectmen and planning commissions in all Vermont's municipalities. Already enough enthusiam has surfaced for the State Planning Commission and the Highway Department to join the two foundations in a demonstration project. The book's principles are being applied to several roads in the Woodstock area, and a careful photographic record is being kept. These photos will be turned into a slide and tape show for some further proselytizing. At this writing, a bill is pending in the Vermont legislature which would allow towns to designate certain roads as scenic backroads, and would establish criteria for their preservation and enhancement.

**Lewiston Artpark,
Lewiston, NY**

Client: New York State
Department of Parks and
Recreation

Designers: Hardy Holzman
Pfeiffer Assoc.

Citation: Imaginative
development of reclaimed
land to create a park for
contemporary arts.

Artpark is to do two things: one, reclaim land along the Niagra River next to Lewiston, NY, which over the years has suffered from bulldozers and chemical wastes; two, provide a setting in which visual and performing artists can work and relax while being watched and talked to by visitors. The idea is to expose visitors to both the artists and their work, and to give artists a chance to communicate with one another, too.

In a first phase, using state funds, what is known locally as the chemical dump, a large sulphur pile, generated over several years by a local chemical company, was contoured into a river bank amphitheater. It seats 300 persons for outdoor daytime presentations of chamber music, dance, modern theater, puppetry or mime.

For sculptors, painters, potters, and weavers a wood promenade, ArtEl, partly enclosed by a curved wooden latticework passes over the edge of the Spoil Pile, rock debris, 45-feet to 90-feet thick, boulders and fine shale dumped there during the Robert Moses Power Project completed in 1965. The promenade descends gradually 25 feet connecting the amphitheater with the lower parking area. All along the ArtEl are enclosures in which artists can work while being watched by passersby.

As part of the project, the riverbank, will be maintained in its natural state. Down the bank to a fishing area popular for generations runs a now reconstructed stairway.

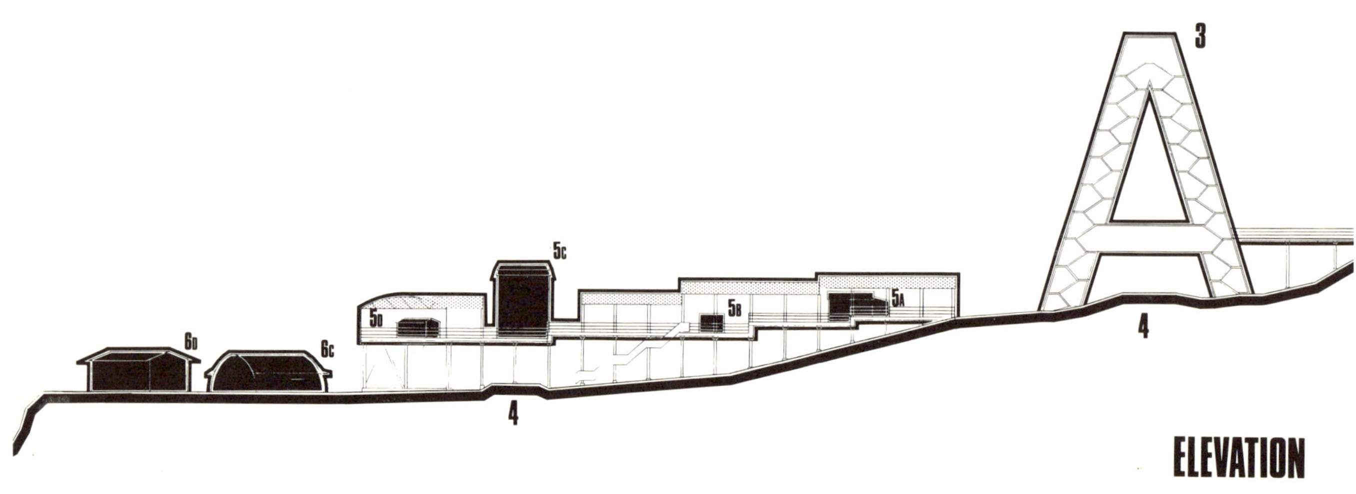

Artpark site along Niagra River (opposite, top) was a chemical dump and a rock pile before development. Elevation (opposite, bottom) shows the entrance walk through a giant "A," the ArtEl where artists will work, and storage buildings beyond. Below are the completed ArtEl and the amphitheater created out of the chemical waste pile.

National Forest Landscape Management Programs

Client: American public via the Forest Service, United States Department of Agriculture

Designers: Forest Service multi-discipline team; Edward H. Stone, director

Citation: In recognition of creating a process of landscape analysis and management goals called visual quality objectives.

The Forest Service is making sure that its employees are aware of the visual consequences of running power lines across mountains, of cutting a ski-lift path, a drainage ditch or any of the hundred other things the Service does or permits. "Eighty-seven percent of man's perception is based on sight," reads a statement on page one of their booklet, "National Forest Landscape Management, Volume 1," and while some might argue with the statement, few would fault their approach to stemming visual blight. While most of the Services's employees are being made aware of these visual management problems, some few are being prepared to teach the subject, and those who will apply these principles in the field are being given a working knowledge of them.

The Forest Service plans a second volume, as a companion text to the first, and there may be more (available from the Superintendent of Documents). Volume One is general, discussing the basic principles of design —color, texture, variety, dominance, etc. Volume Two will be more specific, setting objectives, providing a means of evaluating the visual consequences of land development and construction before they start, and discussing specific problems such as microwave towers, water-system projects and roads.

When trees are cut selectively from the forest, their logging can leave areas looking practically untouched, or at worst with cleared areas (middle photo) which look like part of the natural landscape.

Clearcuts here are unacceptable because they don't look like natural breaks in the landscape. And in photo on the right, the activity is too extensive, totally unrelated to shape and scale of the land.

These drawings show clearcut blocks beneath an open peak, detracting from it. In the after drawing, the clearcuts are reshaped to lead the eye to the peak, making the scars visually more acceptable.

before

after

These two photos illustrate enhancement of the landscape by adding plants which bring spring color (left) and plants which highlight fall colors (right).

Medford Township, NJ

Client: Medford Township, NJ

Designer: Center for Ecological Research and Planning Department of Landscape Architecture, University of Pennsylvania; Ian McHarg, principal investigator; Narenda Juneja

Citation: For an innovative planning approach that starts with environmental resource inventory and results in land-use controls through legislation.

Land-use planning and regulation is one of the imperatives of the '70s, and the residents of this south New Jersey township, about twenty miles east of Philadelphia, PA, and thirty miles south of Trenton, are among those who know it. They had seen what can happen. During the '50s and '60s conventional development consumed the land, creeping east from Philadelphia and Camden. A neighboring township, Cherry Hill, burgeoned from a few thousand in 1950 to 60,000 in 1970. And it bears all the discouraging and damaging attributes of developments in that era — "row upon row of indistinguishable and undistinguishable houses, and miles of commercial strips, interspersed with asphalt acres of shopping centers." They knew they didn't want that. So the mayor and the town residents chipped in $25 per family for a $161,000 study of the area's ecology. It was not to be just another ecological study, but was to be oriented to the formulation of ordinances. Towards that end, the town had some financial help from the Ford Foundation and the Aldrin Foundation of Trenton.

It is possibly the first time such a study (and an accompanying environmental resource inventory) has been aimed directly, as one of the sponsors puts it, "at production of land use controls through legitimate and reasonable regulations."

The University of Pennsylvania's Center for Ecological Research in Planning and Design, in the Department of Landscape Architecture, did the actual study, and they went through the township, cataloguing and evaluating

Hydrology map shows areas of Medford township where water is prevalent. Blue dots mean wetlands. Light blue covers areas which are flood-prone. Solid lines bordering streams means the water quality is poor. Broken lines means water quality is good.

its geology, aquifers, microclimate, physiography, limnology, soils, run-off, management, nutrient retention, potential soil loss, vegetation, wildlife habitats, historic sites, and scenic resources. Each of these was evaluated according to four broad criteria: whether it was (1) inherently hazardous to human life and property; (2) hazardous to human life and health by specific human action; (3) an irreplaceably unique and scarce resource; and (4) a vulnerable resource where unregulated utilization will result in social costs.

The result was a revolution of the planning and zoning in Medford. The town now has a system of environmental impact review, ordinances calling for ecological experts to review plans, and special purpose zoning ordinances, such as controls for flood-prone or fire-prone areas.

The residents and lawmakers of Medford are almost all enthusiastic about their new land-use proposals. Whether they will work is yet to be seen. Brendan T. Byrne, governor of New Jersey, issued a cautious statement on the Medford situation. It reads in part: "The question of whether the restrictiveness of ordinances will constitute a taking of property will rest ultimately with the courts if a landowner feels he is being deprived of a reasonable use of his land. While Medford has expressed concern for its environment and future quality of life, the township may choose to modify some of its initial conclusions when considering its place in the larger metropolitan region."

This map shows the suitability of areas in the township for agricultural production. Colors grade from yellow (suitable land for high value and general crops) to blues wetter lands suitable for certain berries and wetgrass.

A-1
B-1-1
C-1
D-1
35
37
A-2 2
B-2 2
C-2 2
D-3 2
LHPC
A-3 3
B-3 3
C-3 3
D-3 3
24
19
33
A-4 4
B-4 4
C-4 4
D-4 4
24
A-5 5
B-5 5
C-5 5
D-5 5
34
32

Battery Park City Open-Space Plan, New York, NY

Client: Battery Park City Authority

Designers: Lawrence Halprin Assoc. — Lawrence Halprin, principal; Dean Abbott, project director

Citation: In recognition of design excellence in a large-scale open-space plan. The sensitively-handled plan derives from legislation for a special zoning district that calls for separation of pedestrian and vehicular traffic and takes maximum advantage of the Hudson River waterfront.

On nearly a hundred land-fill acres adjoining the southwest corner of Manhattan Island, will be a development that provides space for commercial expansion and, more important, for new housing close to New York's financial district — an area where few people live.

Several things make the plans for this development different, but perhaps most striking for planners is that broad design guidelines have actually been set by zoning law. In the legislation creating a special Battery Park City District in New York are provisions that instruct the planners and designers: (1) "to achieve harmonious visual and functional relationship with adjacent areas;" (2) to separate pedestrian and vehicular traffic; (3) to create an environment that will be "lively and attractive and provide daily amenities and services for the use and enjoyment of the working population and the new residents;" and (4) to take advantage of Hudson River waterfront.

The task was not easy. "How do you knit a raw residential atmosphere with an old financial community?" asked designers at Lawrence Halprin Associates, landscape architects for the program. Compounding the problem was the West Side highway, eight lanes of swiftly-moving traffic that knife between Battery Park City's land and Wall Street. Besides, Halprin Associates could have felt hampered by the legislation. Instead of being given a free hand, they were being told what to emphasize. The solution creates some of the best pedestrian planning done anywhere in the past 25 years.

A platform lifting all pedestrian activity some 30 feet above the West Side Highway is one part of the solution. Bridges are another. Connecting Battery Park City's pedestrian level with the financial district beyond the West Side Highway, these bridges are wide enough for at least one side to be lined with retail shops.

Rising to the platform level, pedestrians cross the West Side Highway on a shop-lined pedestrian bridge. These shops are part of the "lively environment" the zoning legislation calls for, and so are the pools and fountains a little farther on. A cascade of flowing water gathered at intervals in pools will lead down again from the pedestrian level to the waterside esplanade along the Hudson. One edge of this waterfall-fountain will be a school, whose roof is the pedestrian level; on the other side of the fountain will be shops, designed by Battery Park's architects, Harrison & Abramovitz. Though this is the plan for just one of several development areas within Battery Park City, others will be similar.

As a legal district of New York, Battery Park City can float its own bonds and pay its own way without drawing on other city or federal funds. Private developers will purchase land fill parcels from the district and put in buildings and landscaping in keeping with the design guidelines established by the district, and in keeping with the design done in the public areas.

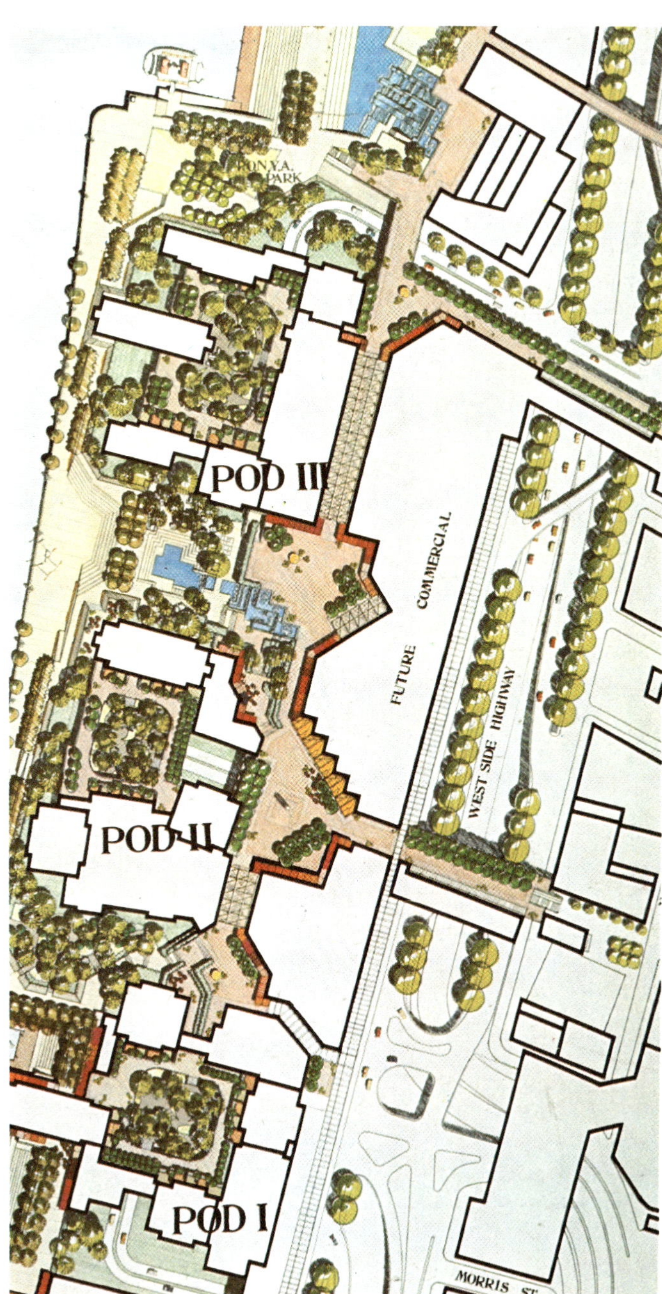

Opposite, excerpted from the designer's slide presentation, are sketches of what the pedestrian will encounter on a walk through Battery Park City.
A — entering from Rector Street, continuing through a public space located 10 feet above sea level.
B — entering from the auto and pedestrian access at Liberty Street, again leading to the Hudson, this time from 32 feet above sea level.
C — walking along the esplanade north from the south cove of Battery Park City.
D — view coming in through the Liberty Street entrance by auto.

Enhancement of Cityscape

Program of Activities for First National Bank of Chicago Plaza, Chicago, IL

Client: First National Bank of Chicago

Program Concept: Gaylord Freeman, chairman of the board, First National Bank of Chicago. C.F. Murphy; Perkins and Will, architects; Robertson H. Short, manager

Citation: In recognition of the enhancement of a major new public space through an imaginative program of free public activities.

The key to the success of the First National Bank of Chicago's Plaza is not its design, although that helps, but its planned entertainment. There is almost always something going on there when the weather permits it, and as a result, it is used by people who throng there to listen to music, eat, people-watch or merely sit in the sun through a summer lunch hour. Arranged on two levels around a square pool-fountain, the plaza has lots of low walls and steps to sit on. Sometimes for concerts or other formal programs chairs are set up next to the fountain, and in the late afternoon the fountain–terrace restaurant moves umbrella shaded tables and chairs outside.

Bank chairman Gaylord Freeman thinks continuity is important in getting people to use the plaza. During the first summer it was open he made sure popcorn was available there every day. And the bank encouraged vendors to sell pop and hot dogs so people would realize they could get food there. Later a high-priced Restaurant Associates operated restaurant, and a middle-priced one looking out on the fountain level, opened. In '74, the latter offered cold entrées and sangria. During the summer of '75 it added hot entrées. And most days, during the lunch hour or evening there was scheduled entertainment in the Plaza. The bank budgeted $55,000 for entertainment and plaza maintenance during the first year, $11,500 during 1974, and for the summer of 1975, it set aside $80,000 (60 percent for entertainment and 40% for maintenance).

Now there are programs five nights a week. About half of these are music—light classical or soft rock. But there is also theater and dance, an occasional sports demonstration or an appearance by a sports celebrity.

These scheduled events may be what bring people to the plaza initially. But once they know it is there, that it is a place to meet or rest, they keep coming back. That kind of continual use is the real measure of a successful public space.

State Street Transit Mall, Chicago, IL

Client: City of Chicago and the State Street Council

Designers: Chicago Dept. of Public Works, Bureau of Architecture, Jerome Butler, director

Citation: In recognition of a plan to revitalize Chicago's main shopping street by eliminating autos while retaining buses and underground transit, and by widening sidewalks. Funds for maintenance will come from a specially created tax district comprising all State Street merchants.

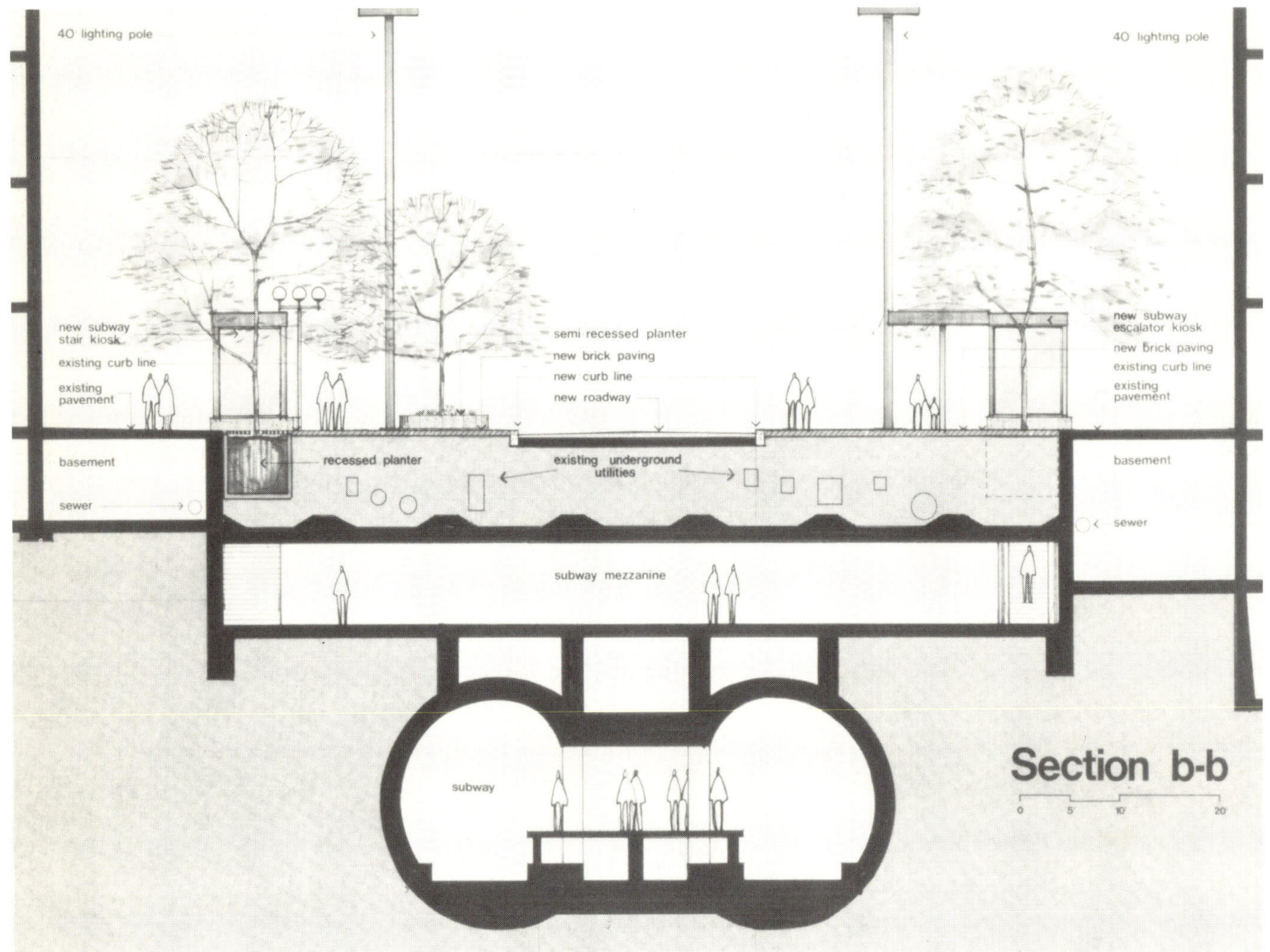

State Street, "that great street," will become a transit mall if plans developed by the Department of Public Works and the State Street Council are fully carried out. A transit mall is a mall where automobiles give way completely to buses, pedestrians, and in this case, a subway. The city is counting on the Department of Transportation for massive assistance — 80 percent of the projected $12.5 million total cost. The city would provide the remaining 20 percent, and the mall would then be maintained by making the area (nine blocks of State Street between Wacker Drive and Congress Parkway) a special tax district, and assessing merchants who front on the mall slightly more than they now pay in taxes.

State Street has long been the retail shopping center of downtown Chicago, and though recently sales there have slumped, it still has remarkable vitality. Mall plans lean heavily towards accommodating shoppers. Some 60,000 persons a day move along sidewalks in the nine block area. Once cars are banned and the sidewalks widened, walking there will be easier. It will also be more pleasant. Not only will exhaust pollution be cut, but also there will be more trees, benches and bus shelters. Amenities are planned to be low-key, playing down to the store fronts. But if the planners have their way, shoppers will be able to stop at sidewalk cafés for recuperation and refreshment. The U.S. needs more sidewalk cafés, and the State Street Mall with its widened sidewalks and curtailed traffic would be a perfect place for some.

Cross section of State Street Transit Mall shows widened sidewalks, subway station kiosks and lighting poles. Specially designed recessed planters have raised edges for seating. Entire units can be lifted from ground to let workmen get at underground utilities.

McGraw Hill Pedestrian Mall, New York, NY

Client: Rock McGraw Inc.

Designers: Harrison & Abramovitz & Harris

Citation: A pedestrian mall, created as a result of new incentive zoning legislation, provides attractively arranged, mini-park space for relaxing, snacking and talking.

Cutting behind the McGraw Hill Building, part of the Rockefeller Center complex on Avenue of the Americas at 48th and 49th Streets, this mini-mall connects the two cross-town streets in mid-block. It gives pedestrians an alternate route, but more than that it provides a change of pace and scene, a brief respite, in a noisey bustling city.

Through only slightly more than 40-feet wide and 200-feet long, it functions partly as a park where people can rest on benches beneath trees, while looking at pools and plantings and listening to the sound of twin water-falls. In fact, one passes through these twin waterfalls, by means of a "moon gate" on a walkway protected by a clear tunnel of glass. When the weather is good Rock McGraw puts out chairs and tables with umbrellas, and a food service sells hot dogs and soft drinks. Entrances facing 48th and 49th Streets are partly enclosed to help screen street noise. And jazz artists perform there.

The mall is the happy result of a zoning variance allowed by the City Planning Commission. To meet its office space needs, McGraw Hill wanted to add ten feet of width to the north-south axis of its 51-story building. The mall is the corporation's compensation for the variance.

BLOOD ALLEY SQUARE
TOYS

GUENTERS
DELICATESSEN
RESTAURANT
EAT IN OR
TAKE OUT
Alexander

Gastown Improvement Program, Vancouver, B.C., Canada

Client: City of Vancouver, B.C. Canada

Designers: Vancouver City Planning staff; consultants

Citation: This historic-area beautification program provides an environment compatible with surrounding turn-of-the-century buildings. Details include a steam-powered clock, brick and stone paving, street lamps from an original 1912 pattern, undergrounding of wires and tree planting.

In 1971 Gastown was named a Provincial Historic site. It is the area which formed the nucleus of Vancouver, the heart of the original city (registered as Granville in March, 1870); it had six buildings then: three saloons, two stores, one hotel. And in September, 1974, an amendment to the City Zoning Bylaw formally recognized the area's "special status" and sought "to ensure the maintenance of Gastown's turn-of-the-century historical and architectural character."

The area had long suffered from neglect, was in fact Vancouver's skid row, but all that is changing. Underway are three beautification projects which have already brought tourists and other shoppers to the area and aided its economic growth. The three are Maple Tree Square (begun April, 1972), Blood (opposite, top) and Trounce Alley (begun June, 1973) and Water Street (begun March, 1975). All are being treated to intricately patterned brick and stone paving, wires are being put underground, trees planted and street lights, designed after street lights used by the city in 1912, are being installed.

There are increased areas of shade, under trees or awnings put up by shop keepers, and spaces for pedestrians to stroll. They can sit on the broad edges of planters or at umbrella-shaded tables put out by restaurants on nice days (opposite bottom). Outdoor restaurants and outdoor retail selling is allowed by the Gastown Zoning statute, but only with permission of the Director of Planning who must consult with the Gastown Historic Area Planning Committee.

Eventually these areas will be integrated into what Vancouver plans as a pedestrian-oriented downtown. Water Street is one block from the Granville Mall and faces the waterfront which will eventually be worked into the fabric of the new downtown. Maple Tree Square looks on one side towards the waterfront, and on the other, up Carrall Street to Chinatown and the proposed Chinese Cultural Centre.

It is indicative of the care being lavished on Gastown, that the signs there are being regulated with painstaking attention to detail. A handsome booklet put out by the City Planning Department, entitled "Gastown Sign Guidlines," states right out that, "Before any sign is constructed, erected, or altered, it must have been approved by and received a permit from the city." This procedure is actually standard in Vancouver, but in Gastown there is an additional step. The sign application must be approved by the Director of Planning who refers to the special guidelines in making his decision. Some signs are prohibited outright in Gastown: roof signs, billboards, directly illuminated signs, flashing signs and animated signs. Other quieter signs are allowed if they follow the guidelines.

Gastown actually dates from 1867. Late that year Captain "Gassy" Jack Deighton, with the help of some mill hands from Stamp's Mill about half a mile away, set up a saloon. It was far enough away from the mill to be beyond its control and sometimes, local lore has it, there were more mill hands at Gassy Jack's than at the mill. Gastown grew rapidly and Gassy Jack prospered. By 1975 he had enough cash to remodel the saloon, turning it into a hotel, which he promptly left in the charge of a cousin while he, Gassy Jack, went back to the Frazer River. Since then Gastown has gone downhill. But it's on its way back.

Waterfront Park, Boston, MA

Client: Boston Redevelopment Authority

Designers: Sasaki Assoc., W. Gerald Venable, Dale Dennis, Stewart O. Dawson, John Adelberg

Citation: A unique addition to the Boston Park system, it provides the only publicly owned "window" to the harbor.

Boston's Waterfront Park might have been only two acres it if hadn't been for the people who live near it. Instead it is more than twice the originally planned size (4.5 acres), and it is a gateway from the waterfront and historic Long Wharf to the greenbelt stretching through Faneuil Hall and Quincy Market to Boston's government center.

First proposed in the early '60s as part of an urban renewal master plan, the park was thought too small by the adjacent North End residents (11,000 to 12,000, primarily Italian) and all the 1,000 to 3,000 waterfront residents. They had checked their facts carefully and bolstered their case by presenting an analysis of existing open space available to the North End and waterfront areas, compared to national standards and the amount of park space in other city districts.

Confronted with this logic and determination, the Boston Redevelopment Authority agreed to increase Waterfront Park's size, then turned to the city and federal governments (Bureau of Outdoor Recreation) for money.

With the needed $2.5 million, Atlantic Avenue was redirected to flow around the park that Sasaki Associates were to create, a park that would satisfy neighbors and other visitors, a total of as many as 1.5 million each year.

Sasaki's solution is a park of several different carefully defined areas (see illustration plans). Rising from the water is a V-shaped cobblestoned plaza, surrounded on two of its land sides by three tiers of terraced lawn (model photo). Here, in this space, visitors can promenade, sit in the sun, or on occassion listen to seaside concerts, watch dramatic productions or wander through Bicentennial exhibits. A large double mast tent is available for these more formal occasions.

Just beyond the tiered swatches of lawn is a lamella wood trellis/rose arbor, which defines the waterfront plaza and acts as a transition to the park areas beyond. At night, says a Sasaki spokesman, "its lights will look like a string of pearls." There is seating beneath this trellis and protected space for an open air bazar or vendors, and boardering it, a pattern of red oaks, giving shade.

Passing through the trellis, one follows brick walks to three other major areas; a large formal lawn, a grove of master locust trees, what the designers call "a formal bosk," and a play area. The bosk has at its center a decorative fountain and a surface beneath the trees of stone dust, an excellent surface for bocci or marbles. In the play area the theme is nautical with a rope ladder, a gang-plank, a crows nest and a shipwreck play form.

Plantings chosen were logically those which thrive in a coastal, waterfront environment. Besides the red oak and locust, there are Norway maple, Japanese black pine, weeping willow and downy shadblow. Shrubs are juniper, northern bayberry, cotoneaster and pfitzer juniper. Ground covers and vines are autumn clemantis, climbing hydrangeas, Boston ivy, and Japanese wisteria.

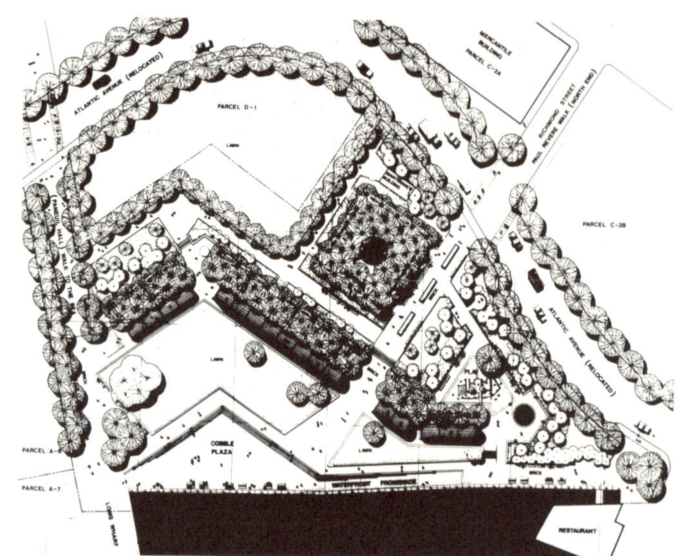

Symbol Signs, U.S.A.

Client: U.S. Department of Transportation Office of Facilitations

Designers: Thomas Geismar, Seymour Chwast, John Lees, Massimo Vignelli, Rudolf deHarak for AIGA

Design of Symbols: Roger Cook and Don Shanosky

Design of Guidelines: Ken Resen of Page, Arbitrio, and Resen

Citation: In recognition of the creation of 34 passenger and pedestrian symbols for use in public travel facilities. Intent is to forestall proliferation of symbols being developed for facilities throughout country.

Though meant to be self evident, readily recognized and understood by themselves, these symbol signs will, at least initially, be used with additional written messages in the nation's transportation facilities.

Once they have become familiar through use, the accompanying written messages can be dropped, and the symbols alone will stand as true international messages, guiding travelers regardless of the language they rely on. In selecting this symbol program for inclusion here, the jurors felt strongly that the Canadian symbol program should be somehow linked with it. Each nation having its own separate signage program is almost as confusing as each airline terminal having its own directional and information signs. The Department of Transportation program hopes to end this confusion, at least in the United States.

As a starting point, a five-man American Institute of Graphic Arts committee, assembled by graphic designer Thomas Geismar (including besides Geismar, Seymour Chwast, John Lees, Rudolph deHarak and Massimo Vignelli) reviewed existing transportation symbol systems. These had been worked out individually over the years for specific installations, such as the Dallas-Fort Worth or the Tokyo airports or for the Munich Olympic Games. But though each had some excellent individual symbols, none of the programs, they concluded, was suitable for use in all U.S. travel facilities.

Citing what they liked in these programs, the committee prepared written guidelines for the design of a unified, coherent set of symbols and called in Roger Cook and Don Shanosky to design them. The symbols, a few of which are shown here, will be used initially in Boston and Philadelphia as part of the Bicentennial celebration and in other test locations.

A book is available from the Government Printing Office (DOT-OS-40192), telling how the symbols should be used in various locations (height, background, color, etc.), showing the sign systems reviewed by the AIGA committee, and giving the committee's design criteria for each symbol.

Client: Canadian Department of Public Works

Designer: Hunter Straker Templeton Ltd.

Citation: In recognition of the commitment to use both French and English consistently and to emphasize, where possible, graphic symbols rather than words.

The Canadian Government wanted a signage system understandable by French and English speaking peoples, one which could be used nationwide in all public buildings and environs, such as parks. With this end in mind, the Bicultural Information Committee of Public Works Canada set up a working group to study the problem. By August, 1973, out of this group's recommendations came an Interim Policy on Bilingual Signage.

The actual signage system was developed by carefully following policy guidelines laid down by this interim policy, by the Official Languages Act, and by the Federal Identity Program of Information Canada. Public Works Canada must insure that the guidelines are followed in both letter and intent. It is less complicated than it sounds. A reference document prepared by Public Works for the signage program shows that these public signs can be standardized visually and bilinguistically.

All signage must be understandable by both French- and English-speaking persons. And to make this recognition possible, signs must be easily identified glyphs, or graphic symbols, or must give equal prominence to both written languages: English to the left in predominantly English-speaking areas; French to the left in areas where French predominates.

The reference manual also gives formulae for the sign's size, shape and arrangement and states what materials will be used and the type of lettering and spacing.

Glyphs are coded in three colors; white on red for hazard or emergency; black on yellow for warning, danger; and white on blue for informative permissive signs.

amtrak

PRESERVATION

Designers and architects contribute importantly to two aspects of preservation: the Recycling of Old Buildings to new uses and the Preservation of Historic Landmarks. Winning entries in this division fall into one of these two categories.

amtrak

Recycling of Old Buildings

Union Station, Indianapolis, IN

Client: Union Station Assoc.; Robert D. Beckman, project director

Designers: Geupel Architects and Engineers; Browning Day Pollack & Assoc.; James Assoc.

Citation: In recognition of the imaginativeness of private investors who are realizing the potential in this. In recognition of the ability of the design team to adapt a magnificent space to new use. In recognition of the city in initiating this redevelopment at no cost to the taxpayers.

Indianapolis's Union Station was designed by Pittsburgh architect Thomas Rodd in 1888. He made it to last, a massive Romanesque structure of brick with turrets, towers and arches. It has stained glass skylights above its 80-foot-high vaulted-ceilinged waiting room; and, in July, 1974, it gained a place in the National Register of historic places.

Other railroad stations around the country are also in the Register, and the listing recognizes their architectural distinction. But they have more than that in common. Most of them are faced with an immediate problem of survival. In Indianapolis, Union Station solved this latter problem in a particularly opportune way.

Awards panalist Norman Pfeiffer of Hardy Holzman Pfeiffer Associates, the architectural firm which recently did a book called *Reusing Railroad Stations,* pointed out that about 40,000 railroad passenger stations were built in the U.S. between 1825, when the first one went up in Baltimore (Mount Claire Station), and 1925. About half of those are still standing, and Amtrack, he says, is getting about 40 calls a month from railroad officials saying they are going to abandon stations.

The National Historic Preservation Act of 1966 has saved a good number of them. The act allows the federal government to match up to 50 percent of the renovation costs for approved projects. But the catch is that the renovated building cannot be used for profit.

Union Stations Associates is comprised of a group of investors who are renovating Union Station for profit, without federal funds. When completed it will have restaurants, specialty shops and entertainment on four levels, and the interior detailing, the grand concourse and the stained glass skylights and windows will all be retained. They are replacing the steam heat with electric heating and air conditioning that can be controlled from the individual tenant spaces, and the skylights are now toplighted. A partial second floor extends out over the grand concourse, ringing it, creating enough rentable tenant space to make the project profitable. A grand staircase carved through the main concourse opens up the lower concourse for tenant space.

One tenant will be Amtrack. In the midst of the new station, the railroad will still operate, although the schedule has been cut from the one-time peak of 200 trains a day to six. Amtrack will also use the station as the northern terminus of its auto ferry system, which routes cars and their drivers by train to Orlando, Florida.

Actually, it was the city that got the right private developers interested in Union Station. In 1971 the city found private interests trying to buy the station, tear it down and put up a high rise office complex. Mayor Richard G. Lugar thought this approach was shortsighted. For one thing, Union Station occupies the site of the first Union Station in the world. Though the present station wasn't built until 1888, in 1853 four railroads ran tracks there, and for the first time, built a common terminal. For another thing, the present station is an outstanding example of Romanesque revival architecture. And the station has an outstanding location, only a block or so from most important downtown Indianapolis buildings.

The city, after reviewing competing bids for the building, merely sold its negotiating position to Union Station Associates, who have saved the building without tapping taxes.

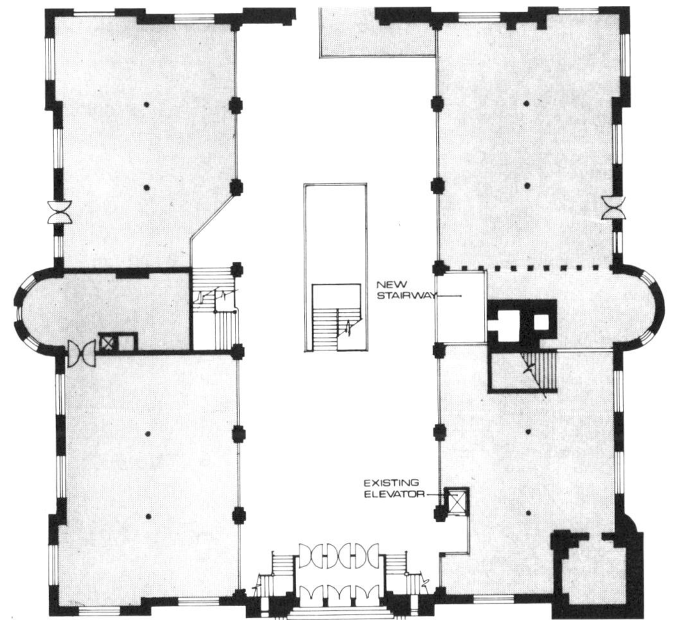

Butler Square, Minneapolis, MN

Client: Charles B. Coyer, Jr.

Designer: Miller Hanson Westerbeck Bell Architects Inc.; Arvid Elness, associate

Citation: The imaginative provision of offices, shops, restaurants and public spaces in this historically significant 1907 warehouse has made it a focal point in downtown Minneapolis.

This handsome one-time warehouse in downtown Minneapolis was designed in 1906 by architect Harry W. Jones. It had 500,000 square feet of interior space in its nine stories, and it was located near the center of the downtown area. Location, just three blocks from Philip Johnson's IDS center, was its salvation. That close to the center of Minneapolis business activity, a building could attract office and commercial tenants, and a first-class hotel could attract lodgers. So reasoned developer Charles B. Coyer who had recently bought the building from the heirs of the original builder, T.B. Walker. (Coyer, though mainly a builder of new office structures, was fresh from the successful conversion of another old warehouse: Canal Square, which opened in Washington, D.C.'s Georgetown section in 1970.)

Coyer calls his twin office hotel building in Minneapolis Butler Square and Butler House, and the two separate facilities (only Butley Square is completed) fit perfectly into the old warehouse because it was divided by a solid brick firewall.

The exterior is brick, too, contributing to its massive look, and because, when Coyer bought the building, it was just being listed in the National Register of Historic Places and designated for historic preservation by the city of Minneapolis, this facade had to be left as it was. Architects Miller Hanson Westerbeck Bell, who undertook to recycle the interior, left the exterior practically untouched, not even removing the patina which had mellowed and aged it. They did lower some spandrels so windows in offices and hotel could run from floor to ceiling. But since the windows they did this to rise recessed in vertical brick grooves, the change is not really noticeable. Inside, the building is vastly different from the dim drab storage bin it once was. Both office and hotel sides of the building now have skylighted inner atriums, created by removing several 14- by 16-foot bays from the center of each floor. The open spaces created are irregular, larger on the lower floors than on upper ones, and in Butler House they will be further broken by room balconies and decks which extend randomly into the open space. Hotel rooms will look directly out onto the atrium, the way offices in Butler Square already do.

But despite the drama of these atriums, the interior's most striking feature is probably its wooden post and lintel support system. Douglas fir columns are 22 inches to the square on the first floor, 8 inches on the ninth. The architects left their wood fully exposed, sand blasting it to remove an old coat of paint, then sealing and staining it. The result gives the building the interior richness and warmth which is its essence. By creating a rised floor system, beneath which run ducts and wiring, the wooden ceilings are preserved.

Charles Coyer thinks "sensitive architectural handling" is at the core of successful recycling of old buildings. But the risks in a recycling project are greater than in a more normal one. "You really can't afford to buy one of these old buildings," he told a reporter recently, "until you've run most of your anticipated problems by the local building department as well as the preservation committees."

Interior of Butler Square in Minneapolis (opposite) has dramatic atrium. Wooden post and lintel support system of old warehouse is left exposed. Shops ring mezzanine level.

The Northwest has a tradition of restoring historic buildings and sites that goes back at least to the destruction of Seattle's commercial district in the fire of 1889. Most of the rebuilding then was done in masonry style a sort of offshoot of the Romanesque Revival prevalent at the time. Today many of these old masonry buildings are being renovated, and Pioneer Square, around which many of them sit, is becoming a part of Klondike Gold Rush National Historic Park (see page 46).

But the Northwest today is known for its use of wood. Timbers and boards, local materials that blend handsomely with local forests and waters, are the hallmark of the Northwest, and renovation there today stresses these materials. Pier 70's typifies the area's awareness of the architectural and historic value of its old weathered buildings — an awareness that was there long before San Francisco's Ghirardelli Square or Cannery made it popular.

Pier 70 might have been torn down if it hadn't been for architect Barnett (Bud) Schorr. Built at the turn of the century, it housed for sixty years, lumber, fish and other goods headed for the Orient from west coast ports. Containerization put it out of business. Unable to adapt, it sat idle for several years while dry rot ate into its timbers and its superstructure began to sag. Schorr was convinced he could redo the two-story interior into a tangle of retail shops and restaurants that would draw shoppers to that part of the waterfront. And he managed to convey his conviction to third-generation owner Edward Dunn. With a budget of $15.00 a square foot, Schorr stretched his renovation funds over a three year period. First a sprinkler system covering the entire pier went in. Next came second-level parking — enough to satisfy city ordinances. Dry rotted timbers came out and fresh ones went in. Then space was laid out for shops, open air markets and restaurants. It wasn't an easy task, walls and floors had warped, and to keep the character of the old pier, both Schorr and the building department had to make concessions. But the flavor of the old, salty structure remains. Sand blasting the exterior helped. So did staining door and window frames in primary colors. By now the exterior has weathered again and Pier 70 looks exactly like what it is: a waterfront structure.

Separated by glass and wood partitions, shops mesh with one another, almost kaleidoscopically, so that standing in one on the first level you can catch glimpses of bits of others on the second level.

Pier 70 could have gone the way of Ghirardelli Square and attracted boutiques which people in 1930 s movies would call "swell," but it hasn't. Architect Schorr, who helped select tenants, held out for counter-culture shopkeepers, feeling they would create an atmosphere that would attract people. But most of the lure comes from the structure itself. In all, there are some 120,000 square feet of space. Slanted glass bays in the pier-end restaurant look out over a 270 degree panorama of Puget Sound and the mountains beyond. It works. Critic Sally Woodbridge sums it up this way: "Pier 70 gives an overall impression of sophisticated but natural design, as sensible as it is sensitive. Despite the extensive recent alterations, it satisfies the yearnings for continuity with the past."

It also provides a needed connection between the citizens of Seattle and their waterfront. They can now stroll, shop and sit in comfort 600 feet out into the sound.

Restaurants (left) and boutiques have taken the place of storage space on Seattle's Pier 70. But the old wooden structure is much the same as it was originally. Owner even moored an old wooden schooner by the pier, as if a cargo of lumber is being loaded for the Orient.

Cleaned and painted, the wonderfully complex maze of tubes, pipes, pumps and condensers (opposite) that once made up the machinery of the exhauster building of the Seattle Gas Company's Lake Station is now a play barn. Children climb over and through the equipment, which, until the mid '50s, helped manufacture gas used in lighting and heating parts of Seattle. Adults photograph it, and everyone who visits Gas Works Park, as the site is now known, can enjoy a touch of Seattle's not-so-distant past. The wonderful 20.5-acre tract on the shores of Lake Union was first put together as a gas works by the Seattle Lighting Company in 1906. But 50 years later it stood abandoned, a victim of the conversion to natural gas. The deserted equipment became a haven for photographers and artists intrigued by the sculptural forms, and in 1962 the city began acquiring the land with the thought of turning it into a park. Funds for the acquisition came partly through a publicly-voted bond issue, partly from the Department of Housing and Urban Development, and partly from the Air and Harbor Patrol of the Seattle Police.

Seattle, perhaps more than most American cities, is actively aware of her heritage, and though the equipment preserved and displayed in Gas Works Park does not date from the early days of the city, it is part of a past era, something that can make people pleasantly aware of continuity as the city grows.

To help the city decide what parts of the gas works should be kept, it called on Richard Haag Associates, Inc., landscape architects. According to site plan and drawings, six generator towers, the pre-cooler towers, boiler house and exhauster building are retained. All other structures had their foundations and apparatus removed and the site was graded by the Gas Company. In a first phase, the exhauster house became the playbarn, the boiler house a picnic shelter. Picnickers now munch hot dogs beneath the drums and pipework of one of the old boilers, and from a recently constructed loft overlooking the picnic area, performers often entertain.

In a second, and in following phases, landscaping, parking, outside play areas and more renovation of remaining equipment will complete the transformation from industrial site to recreation-museum.

Klondike Gold Rush National Historic Park, Skagway, AL and Seattle, WA

Client/Designer: U.S. National Park Service: Gerald Patten, landscape architect; Douglas Cornell, architect; Donald Campbell, park planner; Reed Jarvis, historian

Citation: The jury salutes cooperation of U.S. and Canada in preserving, through passage of historic ordinances, Seattle's Pioneer Square and Skagway, both staging areas for the Klondike expeditions, while also preserving major gold-rush hiking trails beyond the gold-rush towns.

Starting with the Pioneer Building on Seattle's Pioneer Square, establishing and maintaining historic sites in Skagway and Dyea Alaska, and repairing and maintaining the Chilkoot and White Pass Trails, the Klondike Gold Rush National Historic Park will commemorate the Gold Rush of 1897-99. When word of gold in Aláskan rivers reached Seattle and San Francisco, these towns were mobbed with adventurers heading north. Many without funds for outfitting set up offices in the Pioneer Building in Seattle, sold shares in hastily set-up mining companies, and when they had gathered enough cash, set out for the north. Skagway and Dyea (the Chilkoot Indian word for "to pack" or "to load"), just north of Juneau, were the instant cities that received them. Dirty, crowded, brawling, lawless Skagway was likened by John Muir to "a nest of ants taken into a strange country and stirred up by a stick." A Canadian Mounted policeman was more direct in his evaluation. "A little better than a hell on earth," he called Skagway, and, "about the roughest place in the world." Loaded with supplies and equipment, gold-seekers headed for the backwood streams of the Yukon Territory over the Chilkoot and White Pass Trails.

In the late 1890s Dyea had a population of more than 3,500. Then with the opening of a railway between Skagway and Lake Bennett on the other side of White Pass, Dyea became a ghost town. Today you have to search hard on the site for any remains, but the Park Service plans to erect some sort of a structure there and put up historic plaques. In Skagway their task will include preservation of some of the still-standing buildings dating from the late 1890s. Within a Skagway Historic District the town will be recreated, and historic displays tell of the town's history and of what lies beyond along the Chilkoot and White Pass Trails and in Canadian park units to the north. These trails will be restored as hiking trails, complete with campsites and bridges. And passengers on the White Pass and Yukon railroad will be served interpretative materials. During the first five years after the park is formally established, the federal government projects spending $2,086,000 for restoration and park facilities in Skagway. All work will be coordinated with the appropriate state and local governments and when feasible private capital will be invited to help in historic restorations.

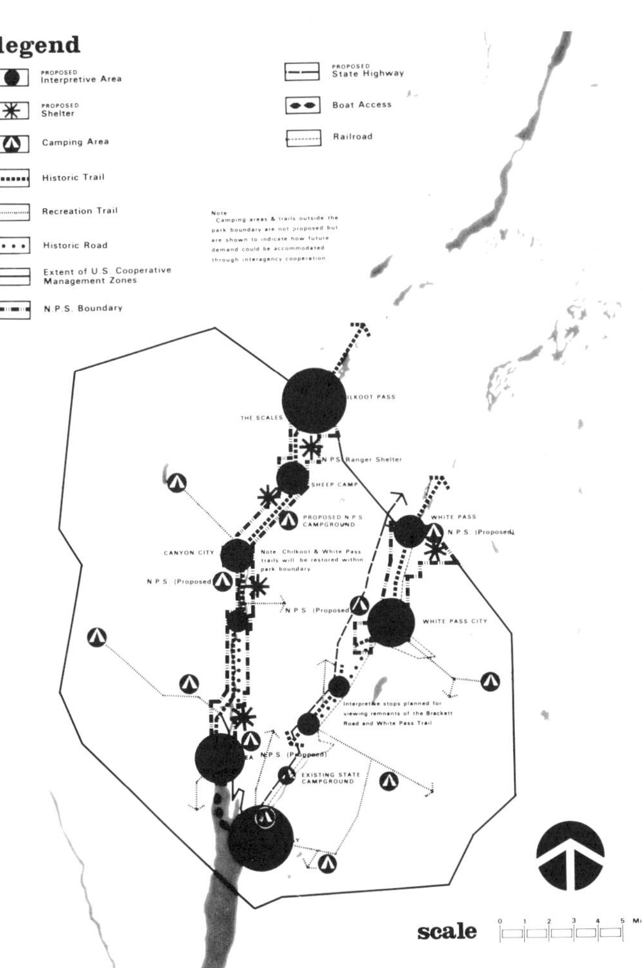

Map shows proposed locations of park campgrounds, shelters, trails, etc. north of Skagway, Alaska.

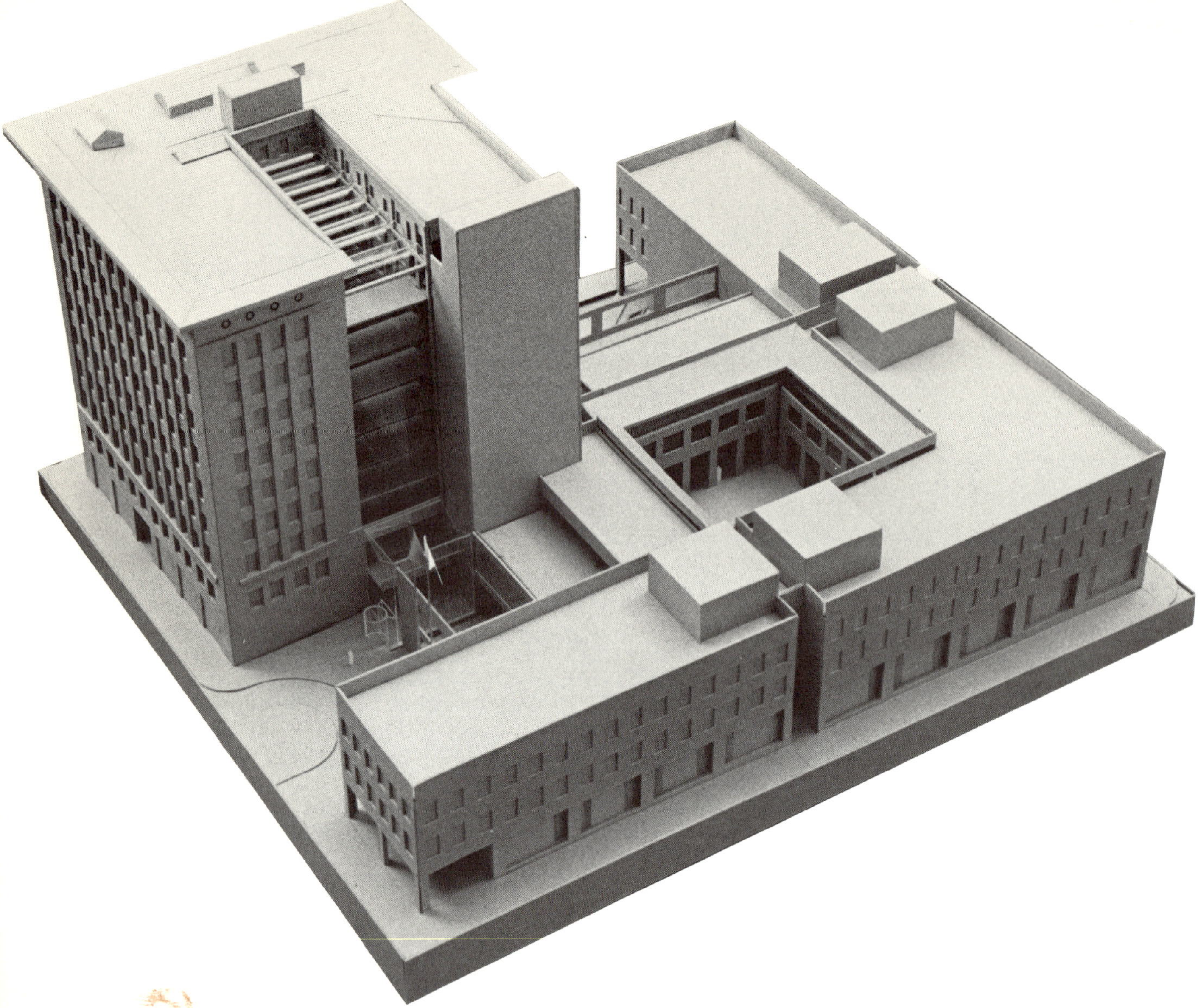

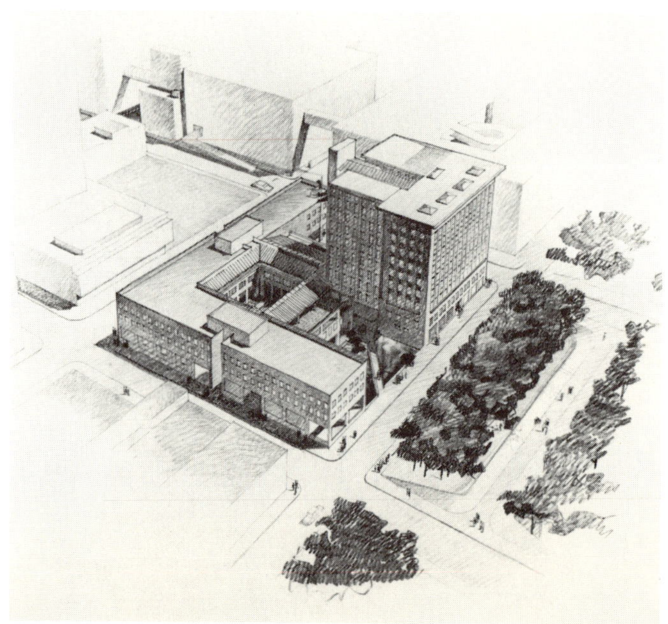

Wainwright State Office Complex, St. Louis, MO

Client: State of Missouri

Designers: Hastings & Chivetta, Inc. — Alan Greenberger, Lorna Katz, Jaimini Mehta, Willie Van Bel, Rick Brown, Ollie Ford, Nurith Bornstein, Marianna Thomas, Lansing Pugh, Sallie Naylor, Nancy Donovan; Mitchell-Giurgola Assoc. — Romaldo Giurgola, Peter Parsons, Brooke Harrington

Citation: The jury salutes the State of Missouri for buying this building and holding an architectural competition in which the winning solution combines state offices with courtyard space. It commends the architects for responding thoughtfully to Louis Sullivan's original architectural statement.

The Wainwright Building (opposite, bottom left) is, of course, an architectural landmark. Designed and built by Adler and Sullivan in 1891 (Frank Lloyd Wright was the office's chief draftsman when Louis Sullivan did the design.), it was the first architectural expression of a steel-framed high-rise office building, one that set the trend in office construction for decades. But though extraordinary, it suffered the decay of any ordinary building. Its offices, originally intended for small independent tenants, are too cramped by today's standards, and it lacks climate control. These things will be altered, while its facade — especially the two terra cotta and sandstone facades with their extensive floral patterned decoration on Chestnut and Seventh Streets — will be restored.

Despite its location — in downtown St. Louis not far from Busch Memorial Stadium and the Mississippi — no one rushed to renew the Wainwright. Developers feared its renovation would be too costly for the return it might bring, and the National Trust for Historic Preservation had finally stepped in, taking an option on the building while it tried to find a sympathetic buyer.

Through the efforts of a Missouri state architect, John Cooper, and Governor Christopher Bond, the state finally intervened, purchasing the Wainwright. They conceived of it becoming part of a state office complex covering a full city block, which would let them consolidate the state's St. Louis offices. To achieve a design that would not overpower the Wainwright, they set up a national architectural competition. It drew 47 entries.

The design criteria were plentiful: There had to be 200,000 square feet of office space, parking for 100 cars, an automobile drop point or front entrance (visible in model, opposite top), and a service or truck access point. Also there had to be open space. When the St. Louis Gateway Mall is completed, the Wainwright will face it (and the proposed General American Life Insurance Building by Philip Johnson), and the state wanted the Wainwright complex to mesh with both the mall and the rest of the city, "to be an outstanding example of urban design."

The Hastings & Chivetta-Mitchell/Giurgola solution shows three L-shaped buildings defining the perimeter of the one-block site (sketch and model opposite). Each is on a fourth of the site, the Wainwright filling the final quadrant, and each L-shaped building defines an outdoor court. Walls of these three-story buildings, left low and horizontal to give the Wainwright top billing, will be of red sandstone. Throughout, they plan to match the color and texture of the Wainwright. And in the new buildings fenestration, they will be reiterating that of the Wainwright's lower stories in size and spacing.

"We are conscious," says one of the architects, "of working with the sharp statement of the Wainwright's form, with the vibrant light of its decoration, with the elegance of its interior and, lastly, with the rationalities and the ironic smile of Louis Sullivan."

Inside, the renovation will more closely match the spirit than the actual detail of the original. (Except on the seventh floor, where what remains of original hardware, grilles, plumbing fixtures, etc. is being gathered and restored). The Wainwright's rear courtyard will be enclosed by a transparent wall and skylight. Courtside windows will be removed and halls shifted to those walls, enlarging the interior space beyond the corridors. By enclosing what were exterior walls, heating and cooling loads should be reduced. Elevators, which some years ago replaced the open cages at the building end of the court will be removed, restoring the original space, and moved to the far end of the courtyard just beyond the building. From there they will serve the entire complex. An exhibit of the buildings history will go beneath a skylight where the new elevator court and the old courtyard overlap.

Citation: To historic neighborhoods in Indianapolis, IN, San Diego, CA, Chicago, IL, Kansas City, MO, Old Gardiner, ME, New Harmony, IN, Detroit, MI, and St. Louis, MO, for important contributions to the nationwide urban landmark preservation movement.

Eight cities (on this and following pages) were singled out by the jury as representative of urban preservation across the nation. Spurred perhaps in part by the fervor of the Bicentennial celebration, communities are finding new ways to preserve their heritage and control their future. Seen in contrast to the abortive, sterile, large-scale renewal efforts of the 1960s, these projects are often small, piecemeal efforts which fuse broader effort. Not surprisingly, they are often initiated by the community. Not wanting to lose their homes (a by-product of much early renewal experiments), residents are taking initiative in restoring their neighborhoods. And they are finding ways of staying put while work goes on.

While the judges did not think any one of the projects merited a citation on its own, together they represent a nationwide effort that is worth supporting.

a. Lockerbie Historic District, Indianapolis, IN

Client: Historic Landmarks Foundation of Indiana

Designers: James Assoc.

Holler Cottage is the first. Eventually its 70 much similar neighbors in Indianapolis's Lockerbie Square Historic District will be restored and renovated too. Like most of its neighbors in the eight-block district, it dates from around the Civil War (1864 for Holler Cottage). Its distinction is that it was so deteriorated it was going to be pulled down until the Historic Landmarks Foundation of Indiana bought it to save it. James Associates, architects, donated their time and expenses to the renovation, and the cottage, now restored (with an added kitchen, central heat and air conditioning), will be sold to provide funds for the district's next restoration.

Indianapolis stands to benefit especially from this work. Right now it has no inner-city residential area within walking distance of downtown.

Holler Cottage in Indianapolis's Lockerbie Historic District before (top) and after renovation.

b. Gaslamp Quarter Planned District, San Diego, CA

Client: San Diego City Planning Dept.; Gaslamp Quarter Assn.

Designers: San Diego City Planning Staff

San Diego's Gaslamp Quarter is a 16-block rectangle, two blocks wide, running from the waterfront to Broadway, between 4th and 6th Avenues. Most of its buildings date from around the turn-of-the-century; predominantly they are brick, three and four stories high, with a cornice line separating a formidable ground floor from the floors above. Many have bay windows. But if the architecture is cohesive, uses are mixed. Dance studios and warehouses exist beside apartment hotels and specialty shops. There are antique stores, bars and bookstores and, near the waterfront, an extensively rehabilitated restaurant.

A group known as the Gaslamp Quarter Association wants to preserve all this, and, possibly, make it better. If their application to make the area a Planned District under San Diego City ordinances is accepted, they would tap funds to widen sidewalks and put in street furniture and lighting typical of the turn-of-the-century. They might, too, be able to prepare a precise design and development plan which would regulate scale and proportion, materials, heights, fenestration and signs.

c. Prairie Avenue Historic District, Chicago, IL

Client: Prairie Avenue Historic Distric Committee; Chicago School of Architecture Foundation

Designers: Preservation-Urban Design; Robert Peters

The Prairie Avenue Historic District is the first in Chicago, and that it exists at all may give hope for the future. Chicago, of course, is an architectural showcase. Most of the leading architects of the past hundred years are represented in the city and at least two, Louis Sullivan and Frank Lloyd Wright, started and prospered there.

Impetus for the district came when "for sale" signs went up on the Kimball, Keith and Coleman houses, three of the mansions still standing on Prairie Avenue, once the stateliest street in town. Already the Glessner House, designed by H.H. Richardson, had been preserved by the Chicago School of Architecture Foundation, and the foundation set up a committee to save the other houses and establish an historic district.

They found buyers for the three houses, then went to Mayor Daley and asked the city to restore the street and sidewalk. He agreed. A state grant and matching city funds are being used to buy about a block of open land surrounding the district's houses. And the city Landmarks Commission is now proposing that the district become an official Chicago landmark.

d. River Quay, Kansas City, MO

Client: The Quay Corp.

Designers: Don Wudtke and Assoc.; Patty, Berkebile, Nelson Assoc.; Saski, Walker Assoc.

f. Historic New Harmony, IN

Client: New Harmony Memorial Commission

Designers: Kane and Carruth; Historic New Harmony

Kansas City grew from the River Quay on the Missouri River, and its history is reflected in many of the buildings in that section, such as the Gillis Opera House, Board of Trade Building, First City Hall and the Pacific House. Now a master plan for the redevelopment of the 32-block area, prepared under the direction of Don Wudtke and Associates of San Francisco, exists, and the Quay Corporation, a private group which sponsored it, is putting $10-million into the redevelopment of the first 16 blocks.

A lot of abandoned space exists there along with light industrial and commercial spaces, and an active central produce market. In a first development phase, groups of buildings within a specific block will be renovated together, giving them common mechanical, fire and elevator systems, and a single main entrance. Spaces where buildings have been demolished will be turned into public plazas lined with shops. Lower floors will house restaurants and sidewalk cafés as well as shops, upper floors will have office and residential space. Sidewalks, streets, and lighting will be restored to their original scale and style.

New Harmony, Indiana was the site of two nineteenth century utopian experiments. Today it has about 1,000 residents, the same as it had more than 140 years ago, and is a Registered National Landmark. A recently enacted zoning ordinance stresses historic preservation, a recently completed Comprehensive Plan sets forth goals for the future. Co-author of the Plan, with Kane and Carruth of Mt. Kisco, New York, is the Indiana Department of Commerce's Planning and Research Group. A community the size of New Harmony lacked internal resources for such a planning effort so they, logically, turned to the state.

Stated goals are, broadly, to keep and strengthen the historic values of the community through preservation and renovation, to have better car and foot circulation, better education, to anticipate growth and preserve the natural surroundings, to have a mix of housing types and expanded medical facilities.

e. A Revival Plan for Old Gardiner, ME

Client: Downtown Gardiner Businessmen

Designers: Ecodesign, Inc.

g. Lafayette Square, St. Louis, MO

Client: Lafayette Square Restoration Committee, Inc.

Designers: Lafayette Square Restoration Committee, Inc.

Small towns have problems too. Residents of Gardiner, Maine, were understandably upset by the prospect of a new Interstate by-passing the city and the highway's interchange, with its inevitable welter of shopping facilities, replacing downtown. Ecodesign, Inc. showed them the dollars and cents value of their old buildings, convinced them to restore and remodel, rather than tear down and build new, concentrating on the typically Maine quality of their town and providing for a cluster of factory outlet stores, like L.L. Bean, selling Maine products.

Ecodesign went even further, suggesting that newer structures be taken down because they are inconsistent with the visual environment. Says one of the designers: "To convince a store owner from a small depressed city in inland Maine to remove the stucco and the 1950s signage from his elegant brick building at his own cost for no reason than to enhance the attractiveness and continuity of a town and to preserve the main street, we feel is a giant step in environmental enhancement."

Lafayette Square, a 25-block area in St. Louis, has more than 200 houses under restoration. In June, 1972 the Lafayette Square Restoration Committee, a group of local property owners, had the area named an historic district. Any facade changes to buildings there now are controlled by the Landmarks and Urban Design Commission. The committee has fought long to preserve the area, once, 140 years ago, one of St. Louis's handsomest residential areas. The committee has successfully had an Interstate highway routed around the district, and it is instrumental in finding both buyers for the houses there and arranging mortgage money for the sales.

Some of the 200 houses being restored in St. Louis's Lafayette Square area are opposite.

h. Woodward East Renaissance, Detroit, MI

Client: Woodward East Projects, Inc.

Designers: William Kessler and Assoc.

Below is sketch suggesting how renovated Victorian houses might blend with new housing.

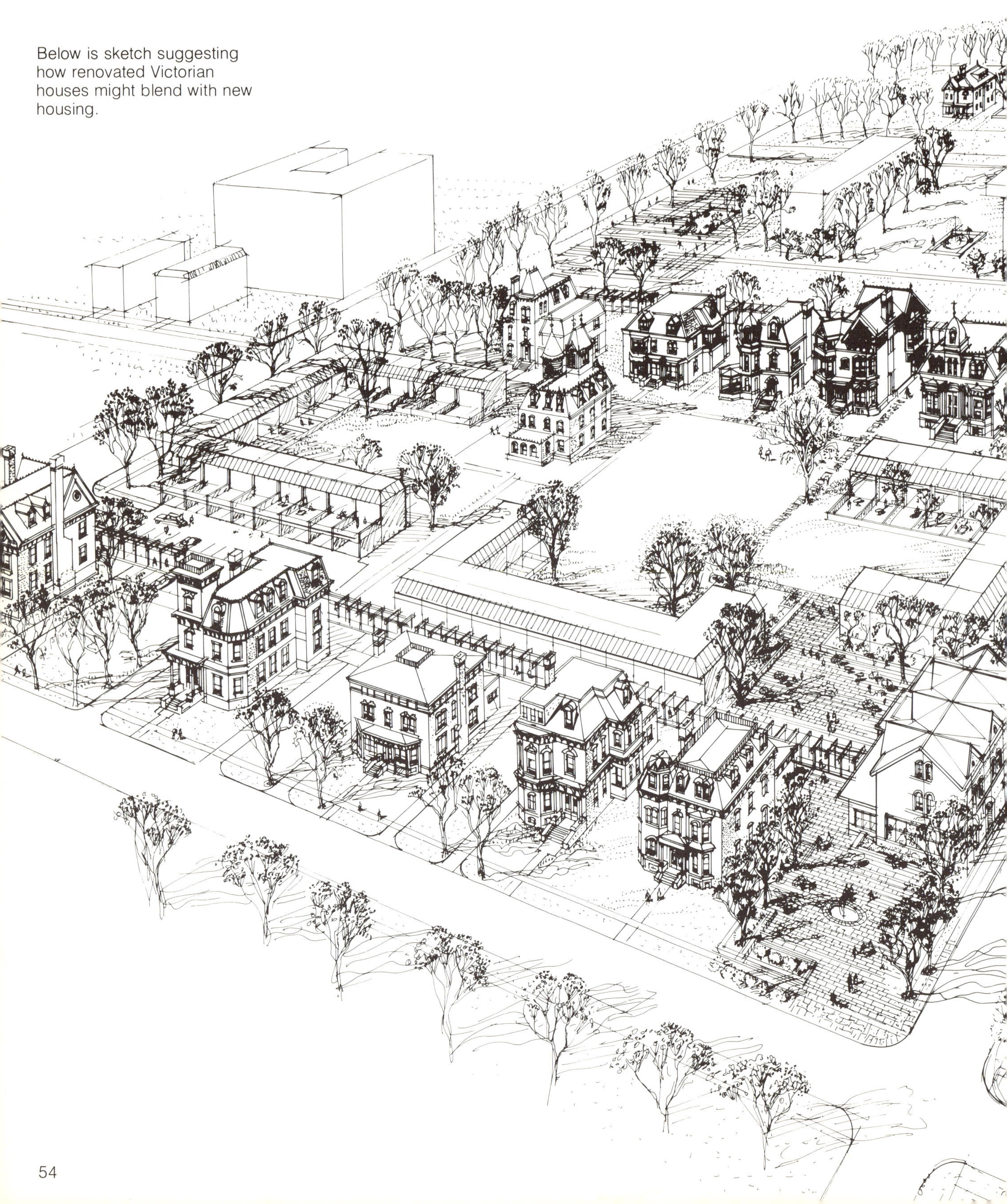

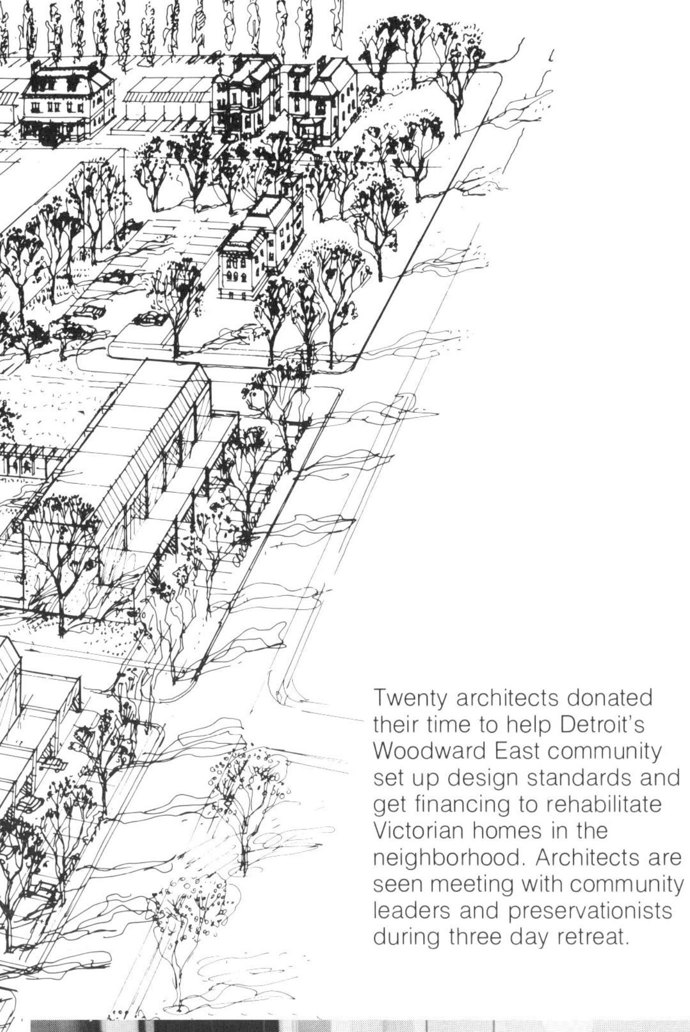

Unlike most urban redevelopment projects which originate outside the area to be restored, this one came from within. Detroit's Woodward East was once the best address in town. Today, income of its residents is the lowest in Detroit. Understandably, the current residents want to stay there, but they also want decent housing they can afford. Playing on the historic quality of the neighborhood, today's residents, through the Woodward East Projects, Inc., raised funds for restoring the area's once beautiful Victorian houses. On a nine-and-a-half-acre site, 18 historically significant Victorian structures will be renovated into apartments. In addition, 104 new housing units, designed to blend with the older ones will go up and some usable open space created. For help, the neighborhood group turned first to professional designers. At a three-day meeting, twenty local and out-of-state architects donated their talent to prepare documents needed for mortgage financing. They hope the project will attract middle-income residents to the area and will stimulate further private and public activity there.

By having the area declared an historic district by state and federal governments, Woodward qualified for government money. So far, funds have been given by state, federal, and local governments, and additional funds have come from the National Endowment for the Arts, the National Trust for Historic Preservation and from private sources in the community.

Twenty architects donated their time to help Detroit's Woodward East community set up design standards and get financing to rehabilitate Victorian homes in the neighborhood. Architects are seen meeting with community leaders and preservationists during three day retreat.

Manchester Restoration Program, Pittsburgh, PA

Client: Pittsburgh Urban Redevelopment Authority

Program Concept: Pittsburgh History and Landmarks Foundation — Arthur Ziegler, director

Designers: Robert Murray Assoc.; Pierucci & Stafanovich

Citation: This program is remarkable because it is the first urban renewal program in the United States based upon historic preservation of architecturally significant houses for low-income people.

The urban redevelopment programs of the '60s created almost as many problems as they solved. Clearing urban areas to put up apartment slabs was inhuman said many critics, and too often people who had been uprooted and shuffled around to live in them concurred. Neighborhoods were destroyed and so was a good deal of historically-significant housing. Now, through the efforts of an imaginative, resourceful group — the Pittsburgh History and Landmarks Foundation — an alternative may be emerging.

Operating since 1964 in the Pittsburgh area, the PHLF has helped restore more than two dozen old residences, a handful of significant landmark structures, such as the North Side Post Office, and perhaps more importantly, has preserved much restored housing for low-income tenants who lived there. Over the years, Arthur Ziegler, director of and moving force behind the PHLF, has refined his techniques. The latest of his innovations is being put to work in Pittsburgh's inner-city Manchester residential area which contains the city's best collection of Victorian residential buildings.

In this essentially black ghetto area, the foundation, joined by Pittsburgh's Urban Redevelopment Authority, is undertaking what they call, "the first urban renewal program in the United States for poor people." First the foundation went through the area grading buildings according to their architectural value, the way a teacher might grade exam papers: A, B, C and D. Next, singling out As and Bs for priority attention, the foundation arranged for the URA to acquire facade easements and restore those facades, under foundation supervision, at no cost to the owners. Owners of the buildings can get a loan or grant from HUD under its 312 loan and grant program to improve the interiors. Work can go on while the people continue to live in the buildings, and, just as important, they do some of the work themselves.

The PHLF hopes that by restoring civic pride to the area, private interests will continue the restoration. Says a spokesman: "Rather than telling residents that their community is so deteriorated that it must be removed (and them removed with it), the public agency and the non-profit organization have united to say to residents that their community is so significant that it must be saved and restored." It is no surprise to learn that residents voted for the program unanimously.

Eventually the funding will go further. PHLF and a citizen's organization are forming a limited partnership corporation, which can act to bring private investment capital to Manchester for home-restoration. Three techniques will make it possible for the corporation to rent or sell these restored houses at low prices:

1. URA's investment in exterior restoration becomes a subsidy for resale.

2. Investors will be permitted an accelerated five year depreciation in housing restorations for low-income people.

3. Under Section 8 of the Community Development Assistance Act of 1974, a number of these units can be rented to low-income people with a HUD-supplied supplement.

So far, 10 houses have been restored, and if the program works well, it will mean a new life for Manchester and also for other low-income communities.

Arthur Ziegler (opposite) is the innovative force behind restoration of the houses seen here. They all are in Pittsburgh's Manchester district, and they are being renovated with HUD money while tenants continue to live in them.

URBAN DESIGN AND PLANNING

To call attention to lived-in as well as planned projects, we divide this section into two categories — Planned Projects and Lived-in Environments.

Galleria, New York, NY

Client: Madison Equities

Designer: David Kenneth Specter

Citation: The jury commends New York City for providing an innovative zoning ordinance that permits mixed residential and commercial use. It commends the architect especially for the design of the glass-enclosed public space.

The Galleria is a 57-story residential, commercial and office building in mid-Manhattan which really serves the city and its neighborhood, not just its own tenants. Probably its most striking feature is a galleria extending through the block between 57th and 58th Streets. Lined by shops, it opens at mid-block into a 100-foot-high skylighted atrium, bordered by a multi-level café (also skylighted), five stories of offices and three stories of a private club with a glass-enclosed swimming pool dining rooms, sauna and gym. This atrium (opposite) is a truly dramatic space with granite-covered surfaces moving diagonally as well as horizontally and vertically. On some levels corridors are open to the atrium, and spanning it are bridges which carry tenants and visitors to the elevator lobby of the 57-story apartment building on the north side of the site.

This mixture of offices and residences required a special zoning regulation worked out between the building's owner, Madison Equities, and the Mayor's Office of Midtown Planning and Development.

Fortunately their interests dovetailed. In the late '60s when Madison Equities was assembling the site, the bottom came out of the office market. They had the choice of holding the property, waiting for a recovery or putting up an apartment building. The trouble was that, existing zoning, while permitting a building with a floor-area 18 times the size of the site for an office structure, would allow one only 12 times larger for residences. Ordinarily, Madison Equities could have built a combined structure, one with a floor area ratio of 12 for residential and of six for offices, adding up to 18, but the zoning ordinance for that area was written at a time when combined structures were thought undesirable. When Madison Equities first approached the Office of Midtown Planning, they came at a time when the office was staffed by a group of enlightened planners concerned about the lack of people found in certain commercial districts of the city at night and on weekends. Putting a mixed commercial and residential structure there made sense to them, and they took the problem to the City Planning Commission and the Board of Estimate and saw, finally, that the necessary zoning codes were enacted.

These codes are complex and call for a certain amount of space open to the public if the full floor area is to be allowed — hence, the galleria-atrium. Besides allowing a passage between cross streets at mid-block, the area becomes a shopping and dining arcade that will draw people to the area well into the evening.

In the residential tower, floors 20 through 48 contain apartments designed by the Office of Philip Birnbaum. These range from studios selling as cooperatives or condominiums starting at $30,000. Larger apartments sell for up to $500,000 and more. On the tower's south side the two largest apartments on odd floors have wintergardens, 13- by 13-foot rooms with two glass walls and a glass roof, the first such rooms in New York.

Floors 11 through 15 have spaces for either business or professional offices. The 18th and 19th floors have housekeeping facilities, maintenance shops and laundry rooms. Levels 49 through 51 have fewer and larger apartments with covered terraces, and levels 52 and 53 have three duplex apartments. Part of the 54th floor houses what the developers call a "sky terrace," an area called for in the zoning for tenant use. In approximately 5,400 square feet are areas tenants can use for entertaining, and beyond them, landscaped terraces.

NewMarket at Head House Square, Philadelphia, PA

Client: Van Arkel and Moss Properties, Inc. in partnership with Kravco, Inc.

Designers: Louis Sauer Assoc.; Adolf DeRoy Mark; James Hamilton of Design Assoc., Inc.

Citation: This urban shopping complex has been built with an inward focus to protect the 19th century residential character of the surrounding streets. The Glass Palace, a highly modern retail center, is connected to the Old Court, a restoration of 18th and 19th century houses, by means of a water plaza.

NewMarket at Head House Square is located six blocks from Independence Hall (upper left) in Philadelphia. Head House Tavern (bottom left) was restored by the city in 1961-62. Upper right is detail from the Old Court. Bottom right is mixed-use building on West End, encompassing shops and restaurants in the first stories and apartments above.

Diagram shows components of NewMarket complex. Head House and the Shambles, park area, are owned by Philadelphia and have been named historic monuments.

Philadelphia has history coming out of its cobble stones, and it may be this inavoidable awareness of its past that has inspired it to do so much renovation so well. Now a project is underway there that combines both preservation of the past and planning for the future. A wonderfully open, many-faceted structure of glass and steel (The Glass Palace), designed by Louis Sauer, surrounding a central reflecting pool, will connect with a three-level structure of restaurants and shops with re-created brick archways circling a brick courtyard (The Old Court) designed by Adolf DeRoy Mark. Mark, who has restored private houses in neighboring Society Hill, is also working with the Philadelphia Historical Commission restorations will have shops and restaurants in the court, ground and mezzanine levels, and offices on their top floors.

continued

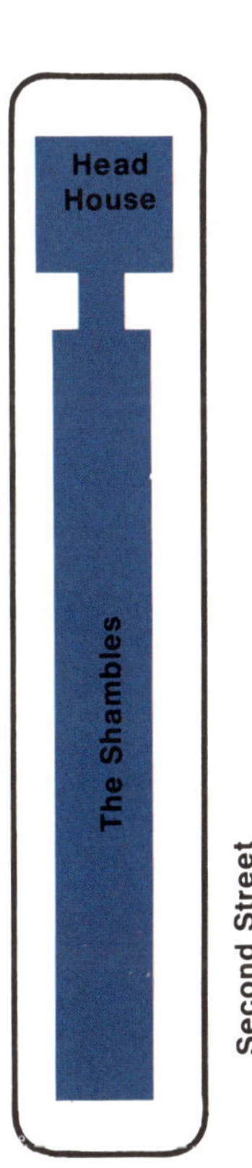

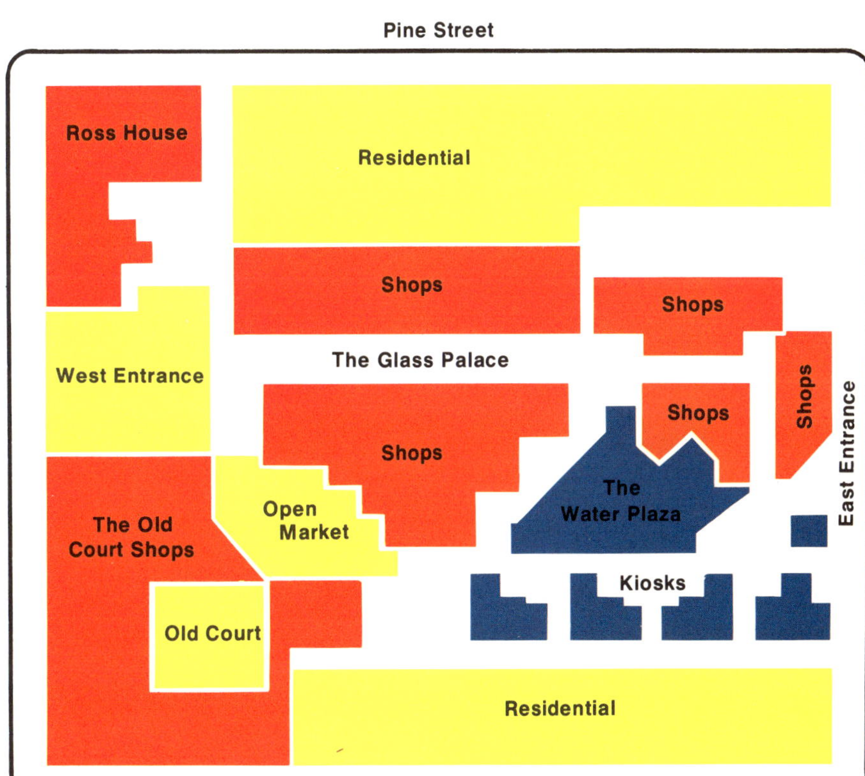

The site of all this is that of an original waterfront street-market dating from the mid-18th century, bounded by Front Street (on the Deleware River), Second Street, and Pine and Lombard Streets. Because of the site's special historic significance, developers Van Arkel and Moss, who with Kravco, Inc., are behind the $10 million project, contributed (along with the Philadelphia Historical Commission, the William Penn Foundation and Kravco, Inc. which will manage the retail end of the project) to a year-long archeological dig on the site. Artifacts unearthed there will be on display in NewMarket. NewMarket is in the tradition spawned by Ghiradelli Square, and will contain in its 80,000 square feet of commercial space, 40 specialty shops and eight restaurants.

One of the nicer touches is a three-tiered waterfall which cascades over oak beams into the reflecting pool. When the project is completed, Society Hill will have a central shopping area, one Ben Franklin could only have approved of.

Head House with its cupola (upper left) stands at the north end of the market. Shops and restaurants are located in restored houses (bottom left). Upper right shows the glass elevator at NewMarket, and early stage of construction of the Water Plaza is bottom right.

Sketch below shows how facets of the Glass Palace and the Old Court will be arranged in NewMarket restoration.

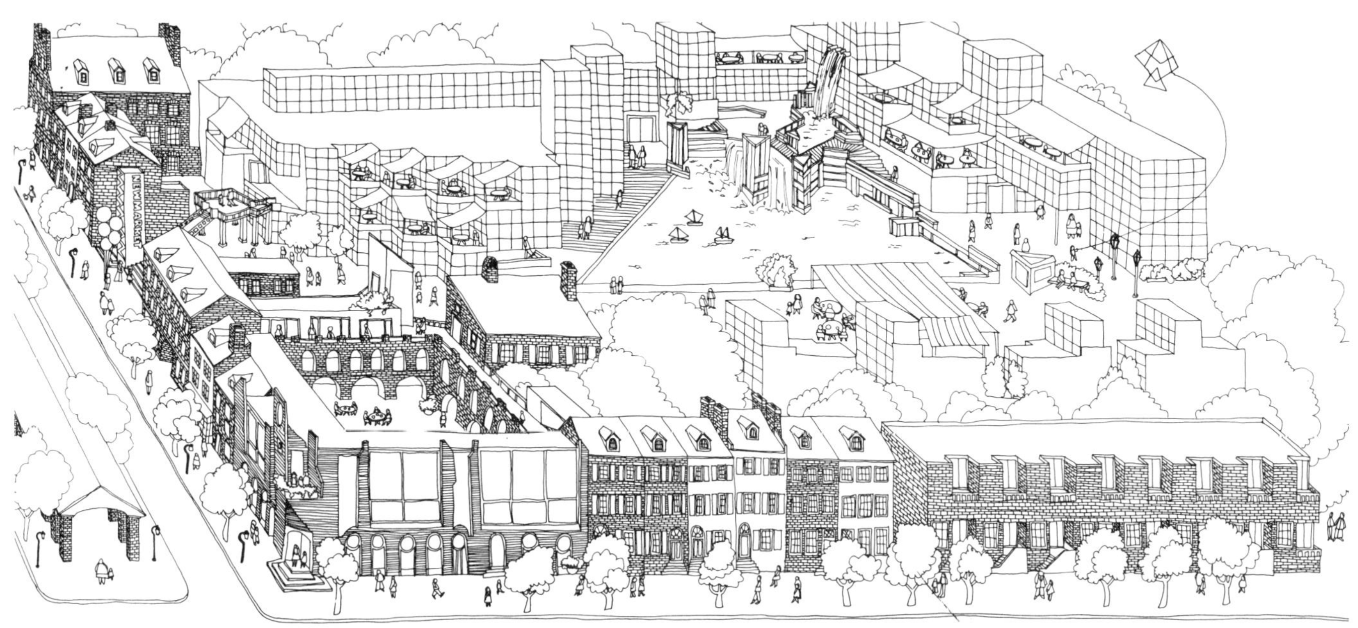

Citicorp Center, New York, NY

Client: First National City Bank

Designers: Hugh Stubbins & Assoc.; Hugh A. Stubbins, Jr., principal designer; W. Easley Hanne, project architect; Bailey S. Silbert, project designer; Howard E. Goldstein, assistant project director

Citation: This unusual condominium development combines on one site a church, a low-rise building containing executive offices, stores and restaurants which overlook a skylit pedestrian atrium, a 50-story office tower, a landscaped plaza with subway access and a through-block arcade. Of special interest to the judges is the below-grade plaza accessible to St. Peter's church and the location of church-sponsored programs of theater, lectures and concerts.

On a full block in mid-Manhattan, bounded by 53rd and 54th Streets between Third and Lexington Avenues will be a 59-story office tower rising from a pedestal formed by four 24-foot-square columns (below). The actual tower, with its 46 office floors, starts 112 feet above the ground. Nestled around the pedestal will be a sunken plaza (opposite), St. Peter's church and a terraced, stepped-back seven-story commercial building with a galleria of retail shops and restaurants. A pedestrian bridge spans the plaza running from street level to the glass-enclosed tower lobby, also connecting with the seven-story skylighted galleria.

By sinking the 9,000-square-foot plaza, the architects shelter it from street noise and bustle and allow it to open directly to the subway. Besides, it relates this way to St. Peter's which will use it for church-sponsored entertainments and events in good weather. Few buildings in New York open directly to the subway, and special legislation, long urged by planning groups, was passed to allow such easy access.

Owners and architects are exploring the possibility of using solar energy in the building under a grant from the National Science Foundation. Preliminary results suggest that the building could save up to 42 percent of the heating and cooling costs of a conventional building its size by using double-glazed reflecting glass and a roof top heat collector, a heat reclamation system and low brightness lighting fixtures.

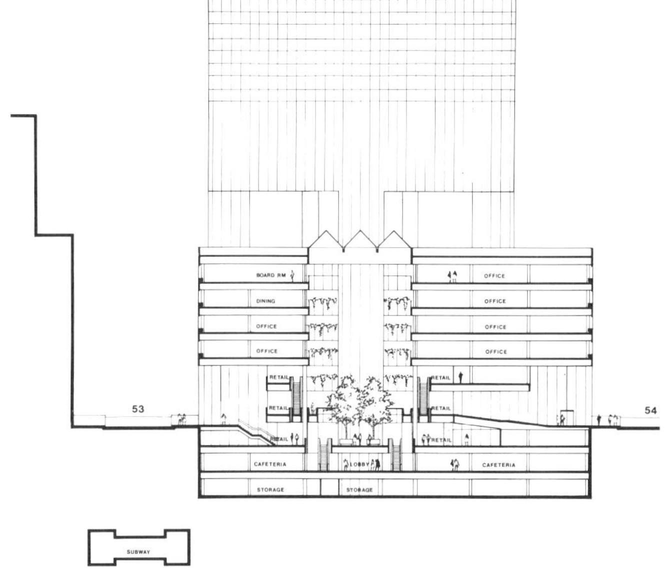

Client: Downtown Advisory Committee

Designers: Barton-Aschman Assoc. — Robert B. Teska, project administrator; John M. Lochner, project director; Thomas O. Payne, project planner/designer

Citation: This organizing concept for downtown Lincoln, Nebraska, includes a planning systems framework for guiding new development and a strategy for implementing a new environment.

In a series of 14 work papers prepared by Barton-Aschman Associates and reviewed continually during their preparation by the Downtown Advisory Committee, Lincoln has guidelines for its future. Downtown Lincoln does not lack vitality. It is the state capital, the home of the University of Nebraska and the site of a healthy retail and commercial community, but the City Council, which initiated the studies, wanted to insure the future. It wanted development to happen in an orderly way, to attract developers to the area who would enhance and strengthen it, and to see that what happened fit preconceptions of their kind of city.

Included in the work papers are a series of plans creating systems — for transit, landscaping and lighting, open space, vehicular circulation and parking — that will be coordinated throughout the center of the city. In addition, they set up a series of districts in which specialized development will take place. Each district will have its own special emphasis but ensured will be easy flow and interchange among them. These districts include such distinct activities as retail shopping, a government-office district, a state capitol district, an office-housing district, and an old-town district. Though distinct, each district could include elements of others, i.e., an office district would have some supporting retail shops, but emphasis would be on a specialty.

Though none of the planning concepts are unique, they will certainly make Lincoln a more pleasant place to live and move around in as its population grows. For instance, plans call for a skyway system connecting downtown buildings at second levels and, in the capitol area, a network of below-grade walkways. Some downtown areas would be closed to vehicles and landscaped for pedestrians only, and two new community gathering places, either open or enclosed, would be created for exhibitions, concerts and rallies.

Perhaps most importantly, the reports urge action now. The city council, the report points out, just denied rezoning applications by three regional shopping centers. What better time to encourage retail building in the center of town?

Development within the districts shown here will emphasize a specialty, such as offices or shops. But of course uses will overlap, and they will all be tied together by common vehicular and pedestrian movement and by a common scale and intensity of activity.

Pedestrian pathways will be linked to open spaces which will give Lincoln a new dimension. When the system is completed people will be able to move comfortably through the center of town, pausing if they like, in parks, gardens or promenades.

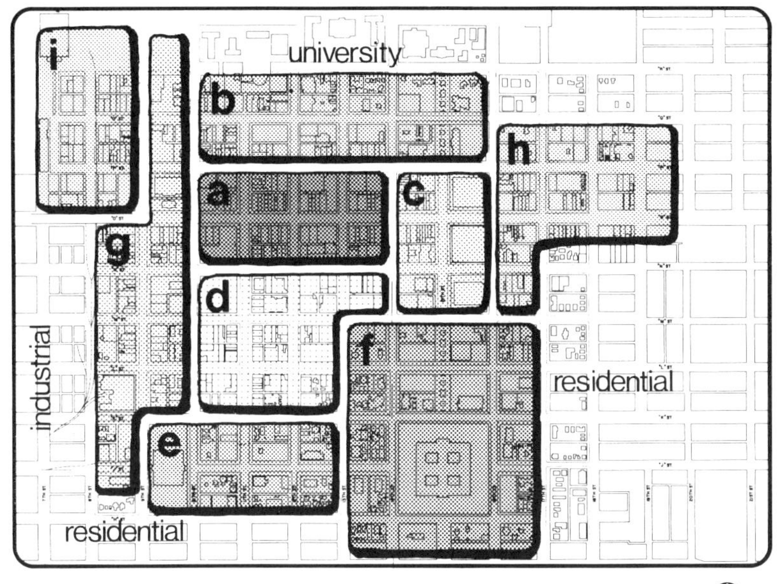

a retail core
b que place
c office-service district
d office and supporting service district
e special office-housing district
f state capitol office district
g auto-oriented regional service district
h auto-oriented community service district
i old town district

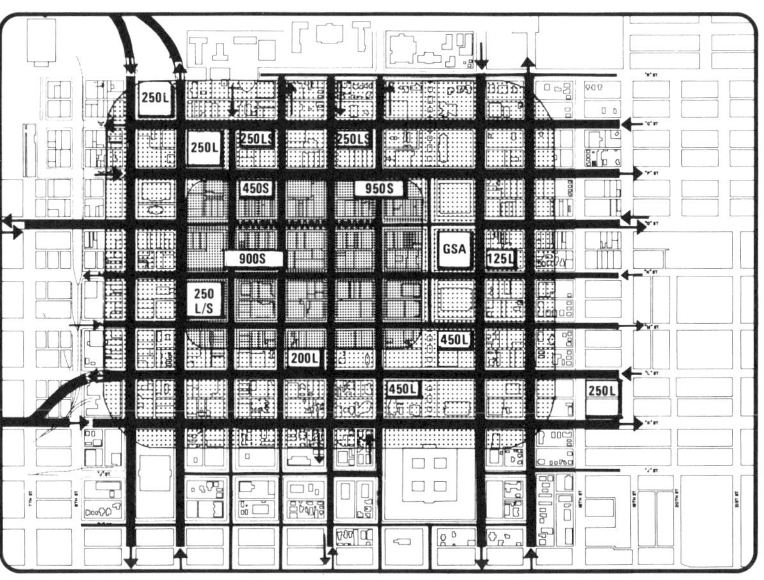

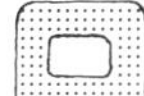

Major arterial street

Minor arterial street

Local street

Special "O" Street treatment

Long term parking ring

Short term parking district

200 L Potential long term parking site

250 S Potential short term parking site

250 LS Potential short/long term parking site

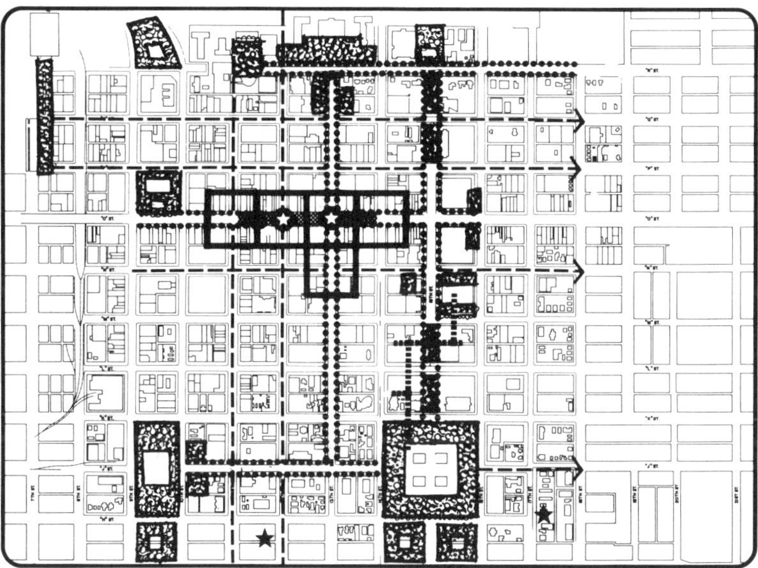

Grade level pedestrian paths

Primary pedestrian street

Secondary pedestrian street

Special "O" Street treatment

Grade-separated pedestrian paths

Skywalks

Tunnels

Open space areas

Central area green spaces

Community "places"

Tot-lots

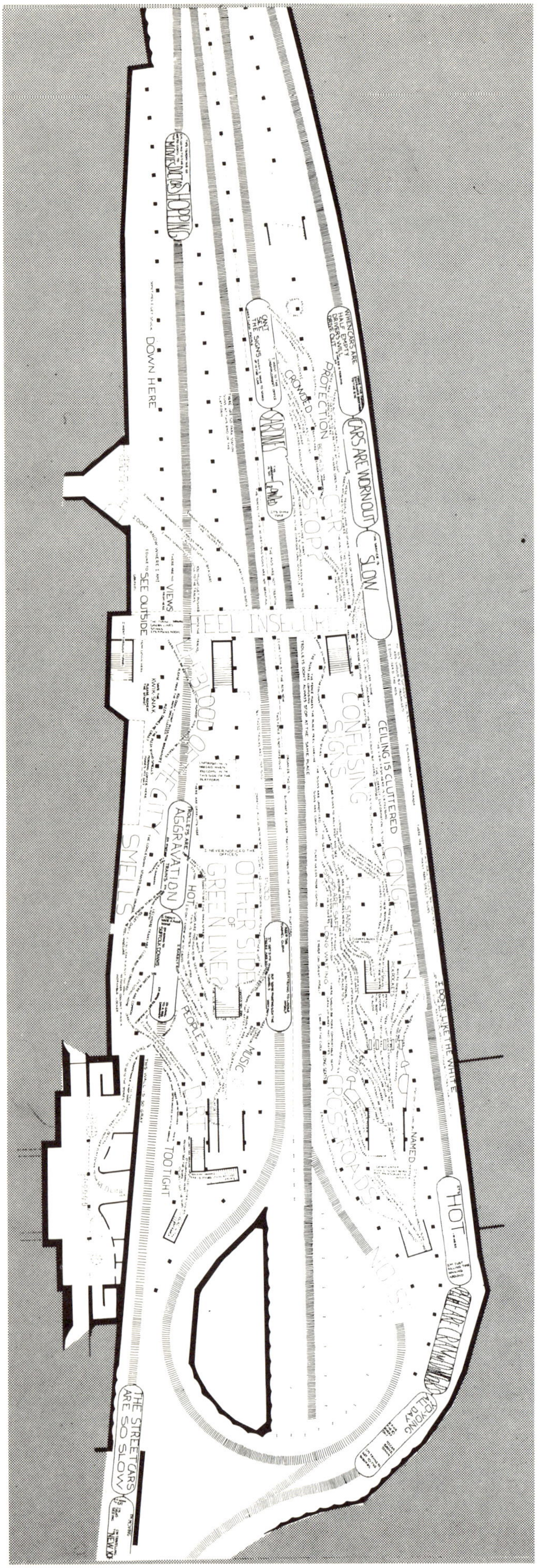

CARS ARE WORN OUT
SLOW
FEEL INSECURE
CONFUSING SIGNS
CEILING IS CLUTTERED
PROTECTION
CROWDED
DOWN HERE
SEE OUTSIDE
VIEWS
AGGRAVATION
HOT
SMELLS
OTHER SIDE OF GREEN LINE?
PEOPLE
MUSIC
TOO TIGHT
NAMED
HOT
THE STREETCARS ARE SO SLOW

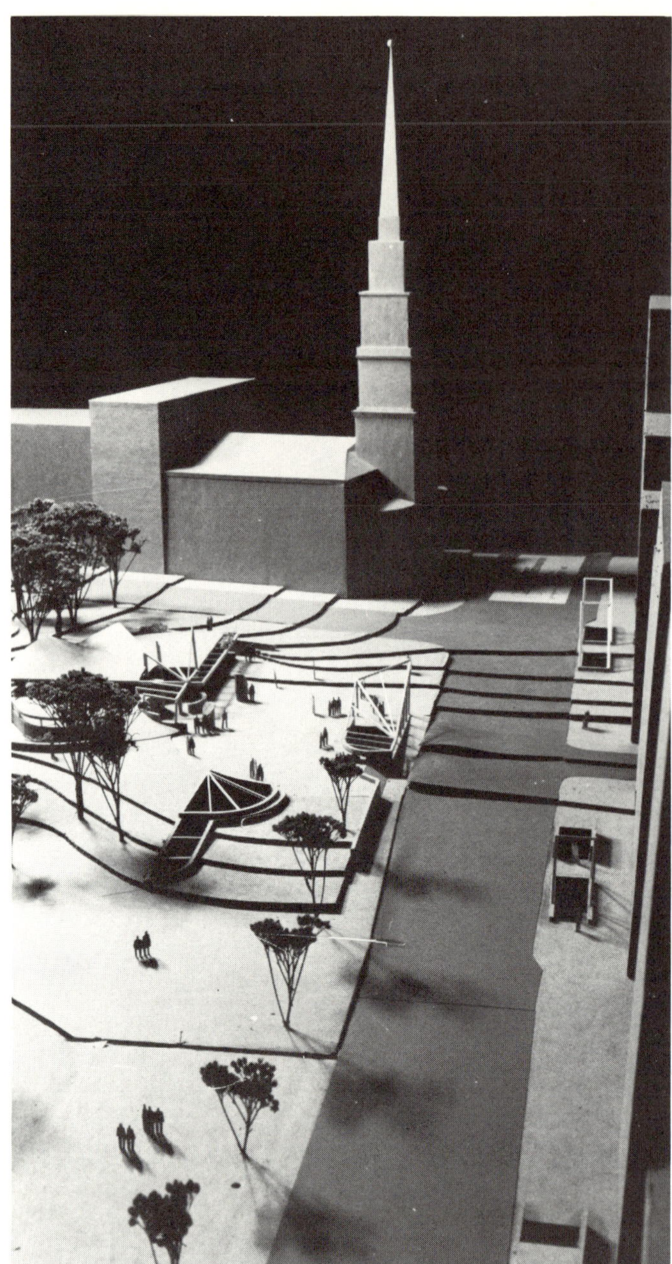

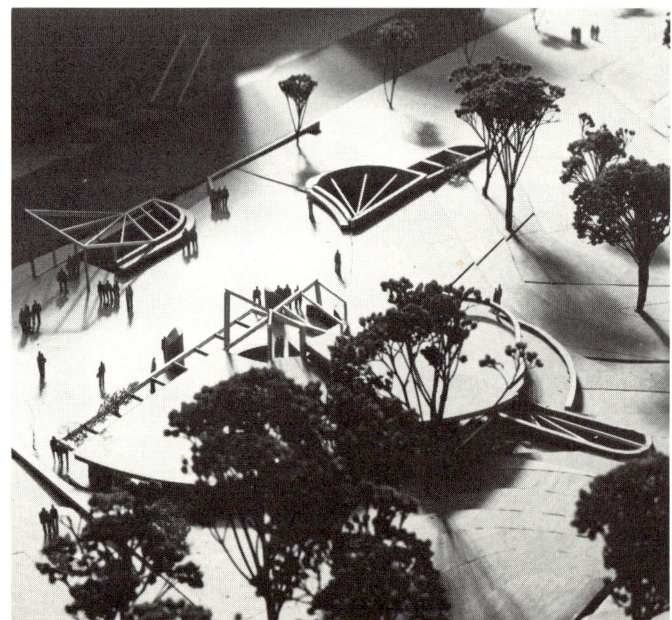

Park Street Station
Modernization, Boston, MA

Client: Massachusetts Bay Transportation Authority

Designer: Arrowstreet, Inc.

Citation: Park Street Station is the hub of Boston's transit system, oldest subway in North America. The station is now undergoing a modernization program, including platforms, lighting, surface finish and graphics. A user consultation program provides background data for the design process.

Boston's subway is the oldest in North America, and the North Street Station, beneath the Boston Common is its central point. Used by some 70,000 persons each day, the station is an exchange point between the city's Red and Green lines, and although it is adequate for the traffic it receives, it is in need of modernization. To this end, the Massachusetts Bay Transportation Authority recently set aside $4.3-million. And Arrowstreet, Inc., the Boston architectural, planning, and environmental design firm, undertook design plans for the modernization. Basically, it will include physical changes in three major categories: (1) better circulation, making it easier for passengers to find their way into and out of the station, pay the fare, and transfer between lines; (2) improvement of the station environment. This will include reducing noise, improving the lighting, color and graphics and providing more ventilation; (3) setting up an information system that will tell riders where the lines go before they enter the station, as well as once they're in it. Also included will be a table of places of special interest or events that can be reached by the subway lines. There may be, too, some provision for a system of advertising, visitor information, and current headline displays.

Wisely, Arrowstreet, Inc. turned first to the people who knew most about Park Street Station, riders who used it regularly. Cambridge Survey Research interviewed 700 of these regular users at some length; then the architects singled out 35 of these who had expressed willingness to cooperate more extensively. These 35, secretaries, retirees, lawyers, housewives, high school students, engineers, an architect and others, were divided into six groups (professional men, women over 35, working women under 35, low-income working people, and people over 60) each of which met four times.

Most of the attitudes of these consultants centered on what the architects call "quality of life," i.e., the noise, ventilation, lighting, dirt, congestion, danger, and lack of benches in the station. Part of this quality seems to depend on circulation, the category next on the list of priority concerns. To an extent, improved circulation may enhance the station's environment by eliminating some of the crowding and adding to a sense of openness. Consultants expressed confusion about just where to wait for trains and complained about confusion and crowding around the turnstiles and change booths. Lastly, they voiced concern about station graphics and colors, both of which might contribute to a sense of cleanliness and light. A good number of these attitudes were put down in writing on a schematic drawing of one of the station platforms (opposite left). Everyone could think of a spot on the platform where an improvement would cheer him and the designers now have a record of these thoughts.

The design scheme is a direct result of these suggestions. Starting with a new entrance building at the corner of Park and Tremont Streets, the corner space will be paved, making it a clearly defined plaza, where street musicians and vendors can operate (see model photo opposite, right). Before one enters the station, one will be confronted by city-wide transit information and graphics emphasizing the station's historic status. Below grade will be more turnstiles then are there now, probably 10, divided into slow and express lanes. And the platforms themselves will be given daylight through skylights which will give waiting passengers a view of the Commons (see model photos). A crossover bridge between the Red and Green lines will give transferring passengers platform views, and, also, the lobby will overlook the Red line, and the entrance stairs, the Green. Escalators will serve both platforms, and an elevator for the handicapped will go in.

Finally, Arrowstreet, Inc. has proposals for modifying the train tracks in the station to gain more platform space and to reduce the squeeling noise the trains make when going around turns.

Client: New York State Urban Development Corp.

Designers: Vitto & Robinson; William Vitto, partner-in-charge; Ira Oaklander, Carlo Zaskorski

Citation: This straightforward approach to urban low- and moderate-income housing is based on a module that allows for variation in dwelling unit types and density. The jury found it a viable alternative to high rise housing in that it provides urban densities but at a human scale.

Using a modular apartment concept they developed in an independent research project, architects Vitto & Robinson propose to stack and align apartment units (sketch below) in four-story rows, on approximately five Brooklyn model cities' urban renewal acres. Their scheme would provide New York State's Urban Renewal Corporation with some 50 units per acre, a density the neighborhood could easily absorb without building any higher than most existing dwellings in the immediate vicinity. In fact, if all plans are realized, the density would be scarcely noticeable. Not only would each unit have a rear yard facing common open space between housing rows, but also two new parks would be created by clearing sites, one just to the north across Fulton Street and one directly west across Hunterfly Place.

Entrances to each apartment would be off these open spaces, and people could gather and children play there without interference from traffic (model photo opposite).

It would be like living on an urban street without the street.

Because the elevated Long Island Railroad tracks run along Atlantic Avenue to the south, the architects propose a 100-foot buffer zone here, which could be devoted to parking. Other parking might go at the corners of the site. Actually two sites are being considered, one (2.1 acres) along Fulton Street, the other slightly larger along Atlantic Avenue. If the land on both sites becomes available, Herkimer Street between them would be closed and used for green space and parking. Walkways would pass through the sites from north to south and east to west.

All housing would be for low- to moderate-income tenants. UDC estimates a total cost of about $9.5 million or $34,000 per unit. Construction would include masonry bearing walls, concrete planks for floors and roofs, and brick cavity walls.

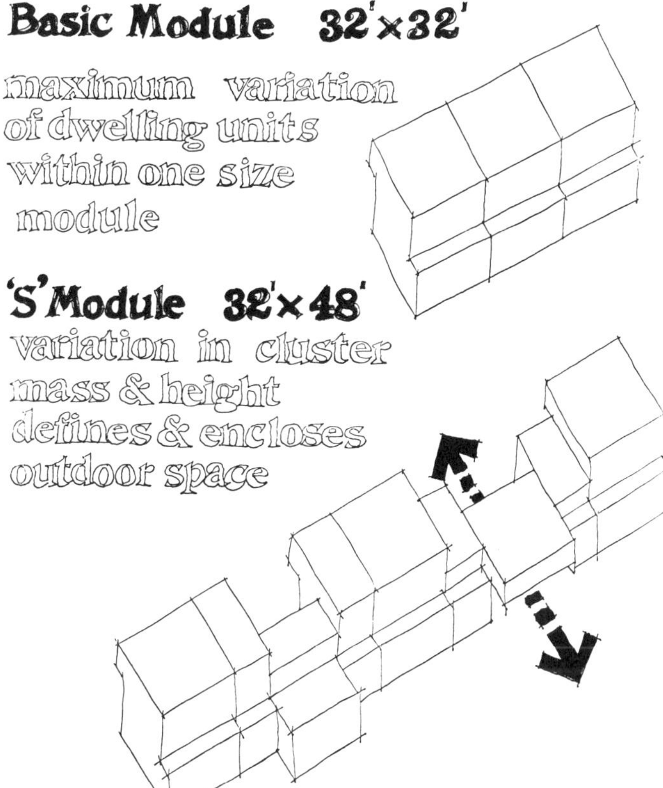

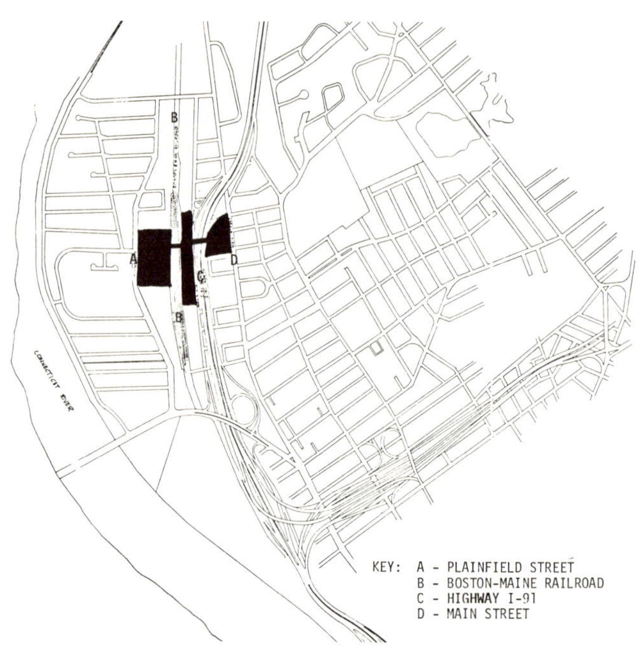

KEY: A - PLAINFIELD STREET
      B - BOSTON-MAINE RAILROAD
      C - HIGHWAY I-91
      D - MAIN STREET

Client: Springfield School Building Commission

Designer: Perkins & Will; John D. Haines, John B. Lodes, John Wainio, design team

Citation: An ingenious attempt to connect neighborhoods cut off from one another by highways and railroad tracks.

Two city neighborhoods in Springfield, Massachusetts are cut off from one another as completely as if they had grown up on opposite sides of a Himalayan peak. Knifing between them are six lanes of Interstate 91 *and* 11 railroad tracks in the Boston and Maine's marshalling yard, *and* a couple of lanes of a commercial street. Whatever ethnic and racial barriers exist are buttressed by the isolation and, of course, such segregation is anathema to today's urban renewal programs.

The solution in this case is architectural, and it is as ingenious as it is obvious — bring children from the opposite neighborhoods together on neutral territory. On a swatch of land between the railroad yards and the interstate highway will be a school for 1,100 fourth, fifth and sixth graders, (diagram, opposite), or at least part of a school. On the railroad side of the project will be the gymnasium, swimming pool and athletic fields. Classrooms, cafeteria and auditorium go on the land in the middle, and in the neighborhood on the opposite side of the interstate will be a park with a fountain. Adults will be brought together, too. In the park will be areas for day care and the elderly. Along landscaped ramps which lead under the interstate, using existing underpasses and new tunnels, will be more day care facilities and a health clinic, and space for adult education classes. Emerging from the underpass, neighborhood residents will find a public library on the first floor of the school (rendering below), and along the ramped tunnel-mall that extends beneath the railroad yards to the playing fields are more community services, counseling, crafts, etc. These underground ramps will be designed as streets, with newsstands, planters, benches and kiosks.

HUD is backing the program, providing $1,781,000 for neighborhood facilities.

Minnesota Zoological Garden, Minneapolis, MN

Client: Minnesota State Zoological Board

Designers: Duane Thorbeck, architect, plus staff from InterDesign Inc. and other specialists

Citation: The first in a new generation of zoos, it creates animal settings from around the world. A zoo ride takes visitors directly to animal habitats, and much is enclosed to allow for viewing even in cold Minnesota winters.

Model of main building complex planned for Minnesota zoo.

On 467 acres of rolling farm and woodland about 15 miles south of the twin cities of Minneapolis-St. Paul, the state of Minnesota plans a new zoo. Animals will be put in areas that recreate, as nearly as possible in the limited space, their natural habitats; and man (the zoo visitors), will intrude on this environment minimally. The idea is to make people aware of their relationship to the natural environment and to let them have fun in the process. It is an ambitious project, especially considering the severity of the Minnesota winter. Much of the area will have to be enclosed, and preliminary plans show vast roofs of steel trusswork enclosed in glass that will cover some of the larger exhibits. Among the major exhibits will be a Northern Trek, simulating an 8,000 mile trip through the Northern Hemisphere; a Tropical Rain Forest from Southeast Asia on a one and a half acre site; a North Arctic Waters Exhibit, which will include a 500,000 gallon salt water

tank with a Beluga whale in it; a Minnesota exhibit of animal species native to the state; and a children's zoo.

Visitors will enter the zoo through a complex of low, elongated buildings which blend with the terrain and house zoo offices, a visitors' orientation center, and eventually a cafeteria. From here they can walk on a raised promenade which winds through and past the exhibits, and like them, is shielded from the weather. Or, they can board a monorail which will circle the zoo, passing through the major exhibit areas.

Plans for the zoo call for it to be research-oriented, and it will specialize in breeding one or more endangered species which can survive in Minnesota's climate.

Design of the zoo's services, facilities and layout was completed by InterDesign, Inc., which also worked out a financial plan. A bond issue will raise funds for construction and equipment.

Model of entry plaza.
Columns rising from plaza
carry graphics that help
visitors find their way around.

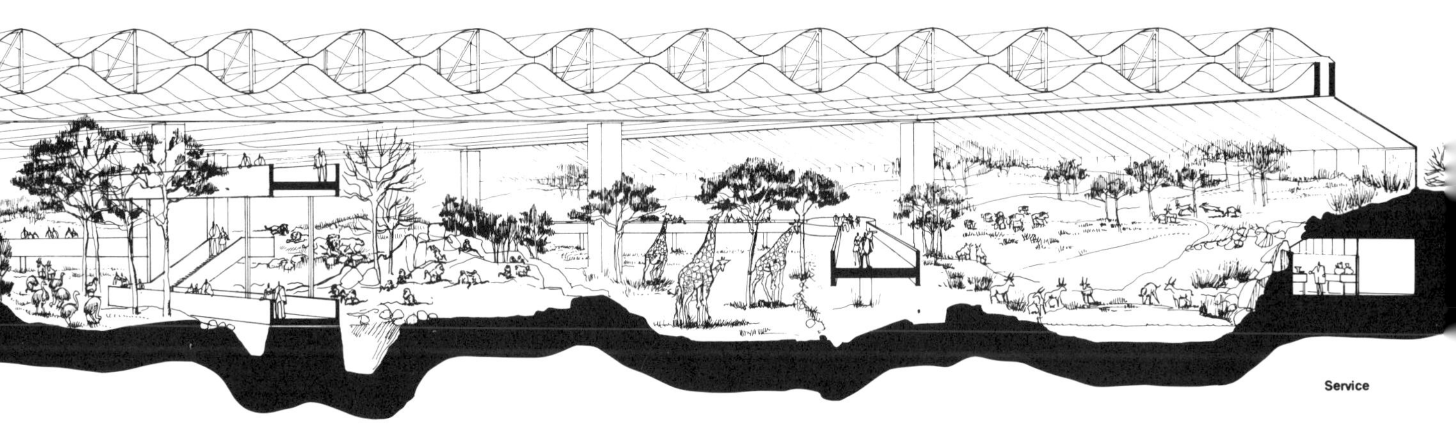

Townoaks Townhouses, Minneapolis, MN

Client: Metram Properties

Designer: Myers and Bennett Architects/BRW

Citation: Aim of the black client was to infuse a deteriorating, racially-mixed neighborhood with a primarily white population that would help stabilize the racial and financial balance of the community. By specifying 14 units per acre, the designer could offer attractive single-family housing near downtown at a significantly lower price than comparable housing elsewhere.

Plan below shows how houses and parking are buttressed at perimeter and center by open landscaped grounds. Project is on two city blocks in an essentially black area of Minneapolis.

On eight urban acres (two full city blocks) about a mile and a half south of Minneapolis's central business district is a planned-unit-development that has brought some middle-class whites back from the suburbs. The developer, Metram Properties, planned this end result after extensive talks with people in the neighborhood. Minneapolis has enthusiastic, highly-organized neighborhood groups, and it is to the credit of both the developer and the neighborhood that the result has been so successful for both.

The neighborhood was changing, losing its racial balance, as middle-class white moved away. To re-establish this balance, Metram offered townhouses at a density higher than the surrounding neighborhoods, but at a price substantially lower than comparable housing anywhere else in the city or suburbs.

Architects Meyers and Bennett/BRW arranged 112 single-family two- and three-bedroom townhouses in what are essentially two rings around an open, central common park. Parking spaces, one car for each unit, are invisible from the street, in an area between the two concentric rings of houses. Although these units are all attached, in a neighborhood of single-family detached houses on 40- or 50-foot lots, the difference is not so obvious as it might be. All the townhouses are fronted by a strip of landscaping along their street sides and each home has an enclosed patio facing either this landscaping or the central commons. Also, the color helps. In a neighborhood where homes are either stuccoed or painted wood with some brick veneer, the townhouses are cedar with battens painted mostly in greens and browns, blending with the trees and lawns. And its facades are staggered fragments rather than lined up like boxes.

The density of Townoaks, as the development is known, is 14 units to the acre, compared to six units per acre in the surrounding neighborhood. Each unit has a full basement, central air conditioning, and an interior two-story, open-stair tower.

When initially offered at $23,500, comparable housing in the Minneapolis/St. Paul suburbs was selling for $1,500 to $3,000 more.

Just what kind of people has Townoaks attracted? These are some comparisons.

Median Family	Townoaks	Surrounding Neighborhood
Income:	$16,000/yr.	$10,000/yr.
Occupation:		
Professional/ Management	70%	25%
Sales/Labor/ Clerk	30%	75%
Market Value of Housing	$23,500 to $25,000	$17,000 to $20,000
Race	90% white; 10% black	30% 70% black

It is also worth noting that 25 percent of the buyers at Townoaks moved in from the suburbs and that 25 percent are employed there, and it is significant that the project was undertaken entirely with private funds — there is no subsidizing. All sales are with conventional mortgages at going rates, with FHA or GI financing.

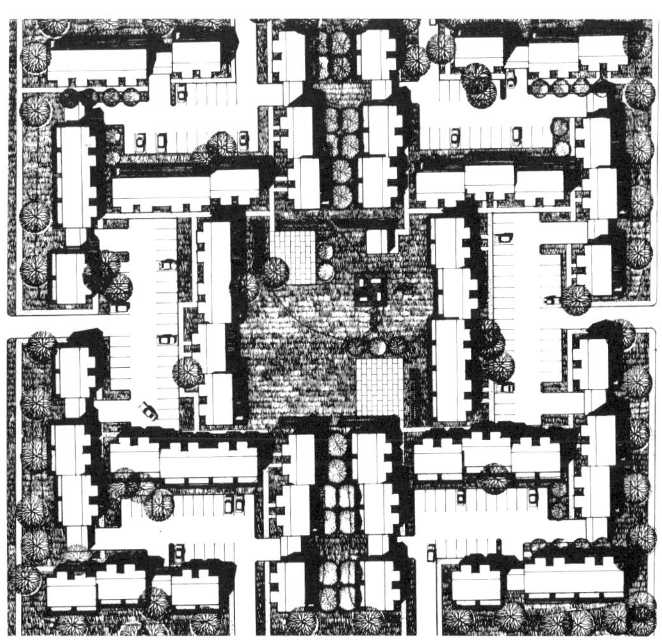

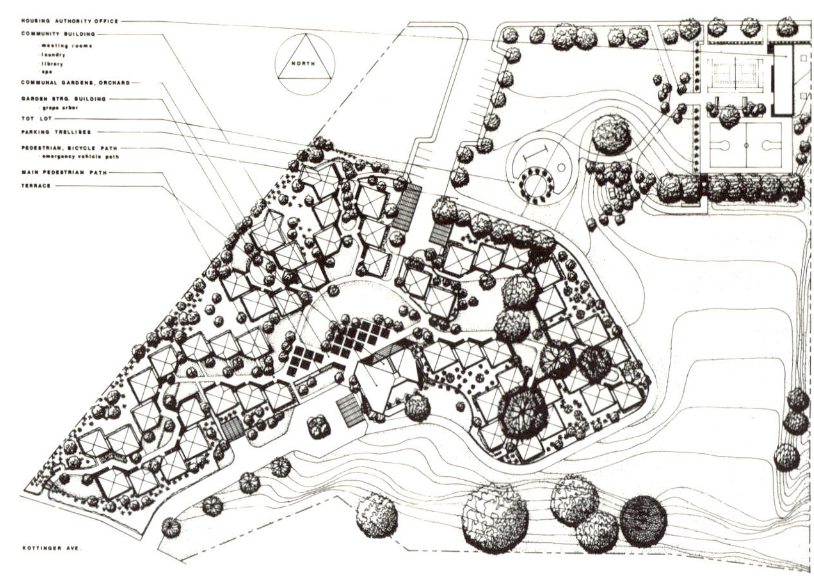

VINEYARD AVE.
HOUSING AUTHORITY OFFICE
COMMUNITY BUILDING
meeting rooms
laundry
library
spa
COMMUNAL GARDENS, ORCHARD
GARDEN STRG. BUILDING
grape arbor
TOT LOT
PARKING TRELLISES
PEDESTRIAN, BICYCLE PATH
emergency vehicle path
MAIN PEDESTRIAN PATH
TERRACE
NORTH
KOTTINGER AVE.

Kottinger Place Housing for the Elderly, Pleasonton, CA

Client: Pleasanton Housing Authority

Designers: Hirshen, Gammill, Trumbo and Cook; Max Schardt, landscape planner; Barbara Cook, social evaluation

Citation: An excellent fit between social needs and physical form, utilizing innovative management techniques and in-depth post-design evaluation.

Before sitting down to design 50 units of low-rent housing for elderly tenants on an abandoned World War II housing base, architects Hirshen, Gammill, Trumbo and Cook went out into the surrounding town of Pleasanton, California and asked elderly residents how they lived and what they expected from a house or apartment. These interviews led to the realization that the elderly, though they have a tendency to become more reclusive, want an environment that widens their scope of activities. They need places to meet, in which to be social, as well as ones in which to be private, and they should have space to walk, or sit and talk to neighbors. Also, there should be places to work, to garden perhaps, or to do carpentry.

Kottinger Place has all these amenities. The one-level, studio, one- and two-bedroom units are grouped in clusters of two or three. From the street they appear cohesive, like neighborhood groupings. But from the walkways within the development itself, each takes on an individual appearance. Each unit has a porch, with low walls and wooden columns, large enough to be an outdoor room with chairs for sitting and a small table for dining. Windows from all kitchens, dining- and living-areas open either onto these porches or onto the gardens and paths beyond.

As one might expect, the weather is pleasant in Pleasanton and residents spend much time on their porches, either chatting with neighbors, gardening (some porches have become veritable plant shops), or just watching community activity.

For those who want to congregate more formally, there is a centrally-located community building, with mail boxes and adjacent sitting area. A large community living room with a fireplace is ringed by alcoves for television, games, crafts and cooking. On a mezzanine is the library. Outside, beyond the large terrace, are the communal vegetable garden and orchard.

A resident manager is available to help with anything from uncooperative light switches to rearranging furniture. But the development's real success lies in its providing low-cost public-housing that preserves dignity and provides community for those lucky enough to live there. Already the waiting list is lengthy.

Site plan (opposite) shows how 50 cottages for elderly residents are clustered around an open space fronting a community building, where mail is distributed and people congregate to watch TV or work on crafts. Part of the open space is taken up by a communal vegetable garden and an orchard.

Each cottage has a partly-enclosed front porch where residents can sit and watch activity on the paths that wind through the project.

Snapshots (above) taken by Kottinger Place residents, show other residents in their homes.

Client: Anthony Capodilupo

Designers: Bastille-Neiley; George Stephen

Citation: By skillful renovation of interiors and exteriors, architects saved basically sound housing stock from demolition. Original tenants have moved back at low rents, and 40 percent of the apartments are occupied under the 236 Rent Supplement Program.

These three-story, bow-fronted apartments on a cul-de-sac in Roxbury, the predominantly black section of Boston, were in the last stages of decay, the result of almost 80 years of neglect. The cul-de-sac itself was little less than a dump filled with trash and with parked and abandoned cars. The area reflected despair, and owner Anthony Capodilupo repeatedly heard the advice that he sell or demolish the buildings which stand on either side of the dead end. These buildings have been in his family for decades, and instead, he took his all-too-common problem to architects Bastille-Neiley for an uncommon solution.

Now, Cleaves Court Apartments, their brick and trim cleaned and patched, overlook a raised courtyard, clean and attractive. There are benches and planters and a Cor-Ten steel sculpture that children climb on. People can meet and talk in the courtyard and park their cars behind the buildings in what was once a muddy, trash-strewn back yard.

Instead of putting up the stark iron fire escapes in the rear, the wooden porch staircases were rebuilt.

Inside they pierced load-bearing partitions to turn some of the 36 apartments which all had two bedrooms, into three- or one-bedroom units, and the space was rearranged to be more efficient.

Capodilupo sought assistance from Section 236 of the Housing Act and kept rents low. Some 40 percent of the tenants get rent supplements under that act. He had to move tenants from the apartments on one side of the court to other housing while the renovation was underway. Then tenants from the opposite side moved into the newly-completed units. When all the work was finished, the other residents gradually moved back.

The project has kept the neighborhood intact and has provided incentive to keep it clean and safe.

Obviously this rehabilitated apartment building on Chicago's South Side is architecturally pedestrian. Its significance lies instead in its solid suitability to its neighborhood at 51st Street and Martin Luther King Drive, and in the care and cooperation that brought it back to life. Built in the 1890s, it had deteriorated so thoroughly through neglect that the city had it slated for destruction. Instead, a development group consisting of Interaction, Inc. (an interracial group of businessmen) and Marvin Myers Associates, decided to fix it up and make it possible for the people already living there to stay. They arranged for financing under Section 236 of the Housing Act so that rents in the renovated building were as low or lower than before, and, more remarkable, they worked out a construction program that meant tenants could stay in their apartments while work was going on.

Like many older buildings, the Cummings is stoutly constructed, and it has many wonderful features impossible to provide at today's prices. "We devoted considerable strategy to saving key elements of quality," says a spokesman for Harry Weese and Associates. And, as a result, oak floors, terrazzo lobbies and bathroom floors, and wood baluster and stairway details are all still there.

Arranged around a central courtyard, the four-story building has 12 segments, each with a separate entrance way, and separate wooden outside rear stairs, shown before and after renovation (right). Each of the 96 apartments has from two to five bedrooms and, as one might expect, the tenants are either elderly or younger persons with large families. None of the apartment arrangements were disturbed. In the courtyard new paving was put down and new play equipment added. The exterior facade was cleaned and tuckpointed, windows re-

placed, new roofing added and skylights placed over each of the entry stair halls.

Inside, the hardwood floors were refinished, new bathrooms and kitchens installed, new doors put up, a new electrical system added and the heating system renovated. Considerable money was saved by putting drywall over existing plaster walls and ceilings. The step took only about an inch from existing room dimensions, and it meant that soundproofing is improved and dirt decreased. And because tenants could stay in their apartments while much of the work was being done, vandalism, a major concern in rehabilitation work, was controlled.

Not only was the work done quickly, but it was also less costly than new construction. And there was an added benefit to the community which is primarily black. The general contractor used minority sub-contractors and employed personnel from a Model Cities program, a federally-sponsored training program for minorities in the construction industry.

All of this worked out. A Weese spokesman summed up the project this way: "There is no new technology or architectural breakthrough here, but the diligent application of sound building and management practices and constant rapport between cooperating groups of technicians and citizens. The pity is that social organization and hard sweaty work are what is most required, not catchword programs and the new technologies."

Another yet-to-be-satisfactorily-solved problem is long-term financing. "State and federal housing agencies seem unable to grapple with long-term (40-year) mortgages," says the same spokesman. "More inventive financial packages must be offered."

Harvard University Undergraduate Science Center, Cambridge, MA

Client: Harvard University

Designers: Sert, Jackson & Assoc., Inc.; Lev Zetlin; Syska & Hennessy; Bolt Beranek & Newman; Dick Oldham; Burgess Standley

Citation: An arcade helps maximize the interface between faculty, graduate students and undergraduates. The designers also closed off a major street and bridged another with a landscaped overpass, thus linking Harvard's north and south campus with traffic-free connectors and adding much needed open space.

The problem José Luis Sert and his colleagues faced in designing an undergraduate science center for Harvard was to make the complex blend with both the university and the town. Sert maintains that "an urban campus is a cultural center within a city and should set an example of good planning and good design for the city. It is, in a way, a micro-city, and its urbanity is the expression of a better, more civilized way of life." Cambridge, while a highly civilized community, has less than half the open space recommended for U.S. cities of its size.

Sert had long been involved in Harvard's future planning. As a consultant to the University Planning Office, he participated in the 8 to 10 years of research and programming that identified the main problems the science center would face. Besides the problem of open space, there was that of circulation. To be located just across from Harvard Yard, the building is a link between the north and south campuses, situated on a full city block, where paths from the two campuses converge.

A third problem was bulk. The center is the largest building on the Harvard campus. It contains laboratories for chemistry, physics, biology, geology and astronomy; offices for the mathematics and statistics departments, four lecture halls seating a total of 1,200, a science library and a cafeteria. All this and more had to go into a single building adjacent to the traditional three and four story brick buildings that surround it. And as if these weren't problems enough, the University asked that a chilled water plant to serve nearby buildings, existing and projected, be incorporated into the design.

All these problems were handled deftly.

In part the solutions to the twin problems of circulation and open space complement one another. Closing off one city street entirely, the architects managed to convince the city to depress another as it ran past the building. The area above this depressed roadway was then covered to become a small park between the center and Harvard Yard. Just as important, the park now means that students and faculty moving between north and south campuses can now do that without crossing a city street or other public thoroughfare.

A prime concern of Sert, Jackson Associates has always been circulation, and in this case the building had to accommodate not only pedestrian traffic within the building, but that through it as well. Two glass covered brick paved walkways forming a "T" make the building an intriguing passageway. Pedestrians are channeled from the street or park into two long converging corridors lined with windows offering glimpses of working scientific laboratories.

"A main street of the sciences," one architect calls it, and it is just that. Bulletin boards become places where students and faculty meet and talk, like the sidewalk outside a small town bank or post office, and a cafeteria, where the two arcades meet, facing a quiet, interior courtyard, provides another more formal meeting place. Part of the idea behind these arrangements is that individuals from the various scientific disciplines might see one another this way, and the same reasoning led to the opening of libraries and lecture rooms off the main corridors. This way the isolation of no one science is complete. These elements are handled with such skill that they are hardly noticeable. What is immediately apparent to a first-time visitor is how the building, the largest on the Harvard campus, commands its pivotal site without completely dominating it. The building's largest single facet, its nine-story laboratory wing, is farthest from the Yard. Instead, a three-story library wing and the small park are closest to the Yard, making the transition an easy one. Then running perpendicular to the library, and the laboratories behind it, a wing housing mathematics classrooms steps back gradually to bisect the laboratories and lead one's eye gradually up to the rooftop cooling towers. Also, near the Yard is the partially-sunken lecture hall element, breaking the rectilinear geometry of the rest of the building, its low roof supported by a space-frame of weathering steel and marine cables.

Most of the building is glass-fronted so you see into it as you approach from the Yard, making it seem less forbidding than it might. Where there are no windows, the facade is precast concrete of a purplish aggregate.

Harvard Science Center (upper center of map) is right across from the Harvard Yard on pathways connecting north and south sections of the campus. Students and faculty will pass directly through the building on their way elsewhere.

Two women walk through the science center on brick paved, skylighted corridor that takes them by classrooms and labs.

Students and faculty meet in cafeteria off enclosed walkway. Science Center is the only classroom building on the Harvard campus with a cafeteria in it. Building is meant to bring people together socially not just academically.

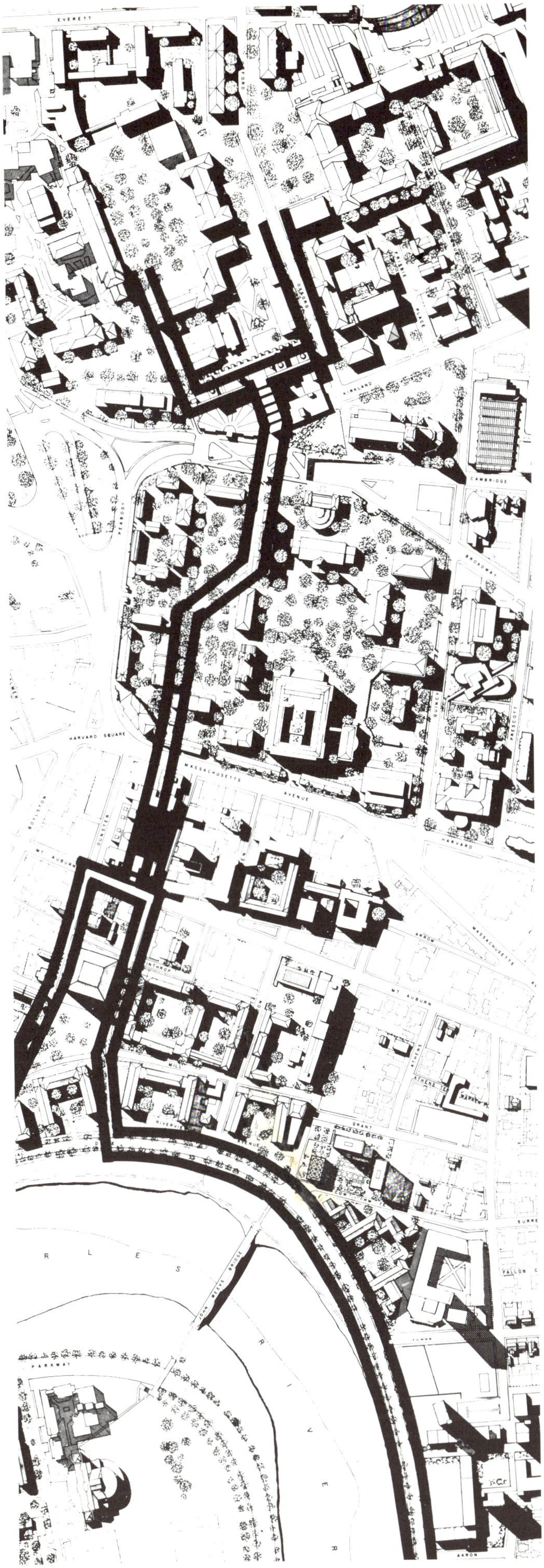

**Programs to Qualify
Residential Facilities for
Mentally Retarded, MA**

Client: Massachusetts
Department of Mental Health

Designers: Environmental
Design Group — Richard
Krauss; Peter Fellenz; Gerald
Robinson; James Batchelor

Citation: Design team
reviewed, evaluated and
planned to quality state for
reimbursements under Title
XIX Medicaid legislation. This
well-conceived, well carried
out process enabled
Massachusetts to become the
first state to quality under new
legislation.

In 1972 Congress passed an amendment to Title XIX of the Social Security Act making it possible for the states to be reimbursed for up to 50 percent of what it cost them to provide certain services for the mentally retarded. Of course, there was a catch in this largess. To be eligible, the states had to prove that their services were living up to federal standards or at least moving towards meeting those standards. Massachusetts saw the Title XIX amendment as a chance to improve its care of the mentally retarded, and in the Spring of 1974 the State Department of Mental Health started work on a substantial report which, they hoped, would make them eligible for federal funds near the end of that year. It did.

Specifically, federal funds under Title XIX go to services in Intermediate Care Facilities for the mentally retarded (ICF/MR). To qualify, each ICF/MR resident must be in an appropriate certified program based on his or her personal needs. In turn, these needs must be regularly assessed and the care program adjusted accordingly. State facilities must meet the federal requirements by 1977 or forfeit the federal funds.

Massachusetts wanted to start receiving federal reimbursement as soon as possible and wanted all of its six state institutions for the mentally retarded to qualify. Moreover, they wanted to start long-range planning, which would eventually give them some alternatives to institutional care.

To do the planning the Department set up seven regional task forces each with this representation: (1) a chairperson from the regional advisory council; (2) a citizen-representative from each area-board in each region; (3) a trustee of the state school in the region; (4) a representative of the parents-friends association of each regional state school; (5) a representative from the Massachusetts Association for Retarded Citizens; (6) a representative of the DMH advisory Council on Planning, Operations, Construction and Utilization.

To assist these regional task forces with their planning, the state then hired the Environmental Design Group, a non-profit architecture-planning firm, which was to help prepare the Technical Plans of Correction—corrections in the institutional buildings themselves—and to provide a report of all the actual planning.

It was a mammouth task, given the few months in which it was to be accomplished, and much of the material is qualified, to be amended later when more information is available. But the DESIGN & ENVIRONMENT awards jurors were impressed with both the approach and the recommendations made for personal living accommodations in the six state mental retardation residences.

Basically, these suggestions were general. The Environmental Design Group recognized the special need for a mentally retarded person to have privacy, a sense of place, and a range of simple choices about where he will be, with whom and when. Sometimes EDG's suggestions were as simple as providing residents with a window they can open themselves or one with a view. Some of the recommendations were in the form of specific drawings showing how institutional dormitory space might be partitioned and divided to provide private or semi-private bedrooms and living spaces for residents. Massachusetts hopes to cut the number of its institutionalized mentally retarded residents in half by 1980, putting the other half into carefully controlled community care programs. So the space made available in the six state residences is ripe for rearrangement. Outside spaces are as important as inside ones, says EDG. By being exposed to an outdoor environment, an environment beyond the confines of his residence, a mentally retarded person is taking the first steps towards living in a normal community. And EDG would remove any reminders of constraint and restriction. Movements can be controlled by placement of benches or planters or changes in level just as well as by fences or railings. Inside, these transitional elements can be much the same, a book case or rack of shelves separating sleeping areas, for instance. And an emphasis is given to providing each area, whatever its function, with as strong an individual identity as possible.

At each of the six institutions EDG selected buildings for renovation and made suggested lists for either closing others or putting them to different uses. With fewer residents, fewer buildings will be needed, goes the reasoning, and emphasis, they suggest, should be put on renovating those buildings to be used so they will last.

In the next phase of the program, detailed design of these changes will begin.

JURY, CONTRIBUTORS AND INDEX

Who Selected the Winners?

The winners were selected by three separate panels representing the three subject areas covered by the entries. The panels met for the better part of the day, each reviewing about 30 percent of the 200-odd entries that had been submitted. At the end of the day, Jonathan Barnett agreed to comment on winning entries, page 6, thus bringing something of the spirit of the awards panel to the book itself.

The panelists worked in three separate teams and evaluated only projects in their own areas of professional competence. The teams and their members (shown left to right in the photos) were:

Environmental Enhancement: Robert Zion, Zion & Breen landscape architects . . . William H. Whyte, researcher, consultant, author . . . Sheryl Handler, Director of Planning Approaches for Community Environments.

Preservation: Janet Vrchota, managing editor, DESIGN & ENVIRONMENT . . . Norman Pfeiffer, Hardy Holzman Pfeiffer architects . . . Kent Barwick, executive director, Municipal Art Society.

Urban Design & Planning: Theodore Liebman, former Chief of Architecture, Urban Development Corporation, New York . . . Ann Ferebee, editor, DESIGN & ENVIRONMENT . . . Jonathan Barnett, Department of City Planning, CUNY.

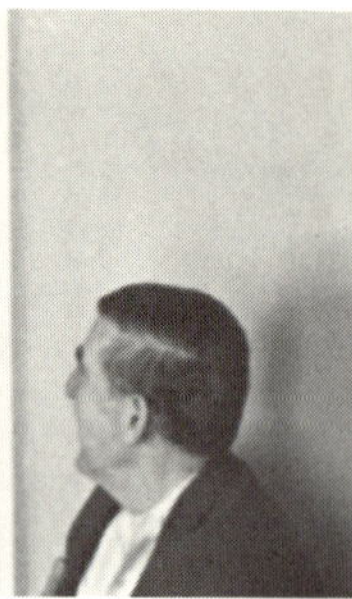

Contributors

Jonathan Barnett

In addition to his work as principal of his own firm, Jonathan Barnett is a professor of architecture, and serves as Director of the graduate program in urban design at the City College of the City University of New York.

Formerly the Director of Urban Design for the New York City Planning Department, Barnett has recently published a book describing some of his work there, entitled, *Urban Design as Public Policy: Practical Methods for Improving Cities.*

Among his recent work as a consultant are development plans for the South Street Seaport Museum, and projects for the Arlen Planning and Design Group. Present work includes Regional Growth Policy studies with The Academy for Contemporary Problems and the Aspen Institute for Humanistic Studies.

Ann Ferebee

Ann Ferebee is a founder and editor of DESIGN & ENVIRONMENT, an interdisciplinary quarterly reaching architects, city planners, landscape architects and other designers.

In addition, Ferebee, who is listed in *Who's Who in American Women,* is currently a visiting associate professor at the State University of New York at Purchase, where she familiarizes students with the best in contemporary design.

In 1972, her book, *A History of Design from the Victorian Era to the Present* was selected by *Choice* magazine as one of the 50 best humanities texts of the year.

Edward K. Carpenter

Edward K. Carpenter writes about design and architecture. He has been an associate editor of *Industry Design* and *Progressive Architecture,* a correspondent-at-large for *Architectural Forum* and is currently a contributing editor of DESIGN & ENVIRONMENT magazine. His most recent book is *The Print Casebook/Environmental Graphics.*

Projects

Clients/Sponsoring Organizations

Architects/Designers

Photo Credits

Perkins & Will   24, 25; 76, 77

Peters, Robert   51

Pettis, Valerie   10

Pierucci & Stafanovich   56, 57

Pittsburgh History and Landmark Foundation   56, 57

Preservation—Urban Design   51

Pugh, Lansing   48, 49

Reed, Jarvis   46, 47

Resen, Ken   33

Robinson, Gerald   88, 89

Ryan, James   10

San Diego City Planning Staff   52

Sasaki Assoc.   32

Sasaki, Walker Assoc.   52

Sauer, Louis, Assoc.   62-65

Schardt, Max   80, 81

Schorr, Barnett, Co.   42, 43

Sert, Jackson and Assoc., Inc.   86, 87

Shanosky, Don   33

Short, Robertson H.   24, 25

Silbert, Bailey S.   66, 67

Specter, David Kenneth   60, 61

Standley, Burgess   86, 87

Stephen, George   82, 83

Stone, Edward H.   18, 19

Stubbins, Hugh A., Jr.   66, 67

Stubbins, Hugh, & Assoc.   66, 67

Syska & Hennessy   86, 87

Teska, Robert B.   68, 69

Thomas, Marianna   48, 49

Thorbeck, Duane   76, 77

Urban Redevelopment Authority of Pittsburgh   56, 57

U.S. National Park Service   46, 47

Van Bel, Willie   48, 49

Vancouver City Planning   30, 31

Venable, W. Gerald   32

Vignelli, Massimo   33

Vitto & Robinson   72, 73

Vitto, William   72, 73

Wainio, John   74, 75

Waste Management Inc.   11

Weese, Harry, & Assoc.   84, 85

Wudtke, Don, and Assoc.   52

Zaskorski, Carlo   72, 73

Ziegler, Arthur   56, 57

Zetlin, Lev   86, 87

Environmental Enhancement: David L. Hirsch — 17; Peter Aaron — 22, 23; Cricket Porter — 24; Harr, Hedrich-Blessing — 25

Preservation: Courtesy of Miller Hanson Westerbeck Bell Architects, Inc. — 40; Rollin R. LaFrance — 48

Urban Design and Planning: Hugh Stubbins & Assoc. — 67; Arrowstreet, Inc. — 70; Robert Galbraith — 72, 73; Les Turnau — 78; Philip Mac Millan, James & Assoc. — 79; Steve Rosenthal — 82, 83; Jim Hedrich of Hedrich-Blessing — 84, 85; Lorie Handler — 86, 87